a shortcut to
perfect planting

spectacular ideas for every season

a shortcut to
perfect planting

rob cassy

For Mum, Dad, Susan and Richard

Published in 2002 by Conran Octopus Limited
a part of the Octopus Publishing Group
2–4 Heron Quays, London E14 4JP
Visit our website at www.conran-octopus.co.uk

British Library Cataloguing-in-Publication Data.
A catalogue record for this book is available from the British Library

Publishing Director: Lorraine Dickey
Senior Editor: Katey Day
Creative Director: Leslie Harrington
Designer: Sue Storey
Picture Research: Liz Boyd
Senior Production Controller: Manjit Sihra

ISBN 1 84091 280 4

Printed in China

page 1: *Convallaria majalis* 'Albostriata';
page 2–3: *Euonymus europaeus* 'Red Cascade';
above from left to right: *Galanthus elwesii*; *Tulipa acuminata*; *Agapanthus* 'Cherry Holley'; *Acer palmatum* 'Bloodgood'

contents

introduction

The works of a person that builds, begin immediately to decay; while those of him who plants begin directly to improve.

William Shenstone (1714–1763)

left: *Dahlia* 'Bishop of Llandaff; above: *Iris foetidissima*

introduction

LIFE IS COMPLICATED ENOUGH AS IT IS, SO I ABSOLUTELY FORBID YOU TO *WORRY* ABOUT GARDENING. Ogle and fantasize, by all means. Go shopping and pick up something gorgeous, certainly. Learn a few simple techniques and mount a fantastic display – yes, yes, yes!

Surely the whole point of creating a brand new garden, or of nurturing and enhancing an existing one, is to find personal satisfaction and to give pleasure to others. Performance anxiety only takes the enjoyment out of gardening. In fact, it makes many a poor soul shrink from the attempt. Don't die wondering – it's perfectly possible to become a serious gardener without being the least bit uptight about plants. So just relax and do what comes naturally. It's a lot more exciting that way…

Leave any patch of earth untended and it will soon be teeming with young plants. The prettier, more unusual ones we tend to call wildflowers, the homelier ones are derided as weeds. Because their seeds are floating on the air and lurking in the topsoil along with bits of root and the occasional bulb, native plants are ready, willing and able to decorate your garden at a moment's notice. Some enjoy basking in sunshine, others prefer partial or heavy shade. Some are heavy drinkers, others are remarkably abstinent. Some thrive on meagre rations, others feed like pigs at a trough. Those lucky enough to turn up in just the right setting for their species are laughing. Happy plants quickly capitalize on their good fortune to form thriving, self-perpetuating colonies by spreading their roots, by growing offsets to bulbs, and by flowering to produce seeds.

Gardening is simply a matter of shutting the door on Nature's prêt à porter collection in favour of haute couture. Among other delights in the following pages you will find peonies the size of dinner plates, a colour-changing rose, an aromatic shrub smelling of blackcurrant cough linctus, chocolate-, vanilla- and honey-scented blooms, a clematis with petals thick as orange peel, and some truly eye-popping berries. The addition of a few stunning plants transforms any outdoor space at a stroke – and anyone can do it. 'Garden' plants come from all around the globe but, in their original form, they are no more and no less than the weeds and wildflowers of their native lands. All they need to succeed is for you to settle them comfortably in a spot that reminds them of home. This is why it is so useful to know the origins of your plants.

Discovering where in the world they come from, then mulling a while on growing conditions in their native habitat, quickly tells you how well they will do in your garden. It also indicates how you might tweak things a little to make them more comfortable in the quarters you can provide. A northern European woodlander will enjoy a cool and shaded spot with a rich leafy soil – so bed it in with plenty of well-rotted compost under the overhanging branches of a shrub. A bulb accustomed to South African sunshine will want to bask in the hottest spot

below: *Oenothera biennis*

available, sheltered from cold winds – so grow it at the foot of a warm house wall. An alpine plant will flourish on an exposed site in free-draining stony ground – need I go on?

All you need for a successful garden is a range of outstanding specimens providing colour, form and fragrance throughout the year. This is why the plants in this book are arranged according to their season of peak performance. Mix, match and run them through each other as you will (growing conditions permitting), to create the garden of your dreams at a dash, or select just a few at a time to create dramatic new highlights when and where you need them most.

All hobbies and professions develop a jargon, which can be off-putting to newcomers but enables initiates to express themselves clearly and precisely. Gardening is no exception. Before going any further, let's run briefly through the basics. Annuals complete their life-cycles in a year, so give rapid but fleeting results. Biennials hang around longer, flowering and setting seed when they are two years old. Perennials go on almost forever; some are evergreen, others are herbaceous and have a dormant period when they die back to the ground. Trees and shrubs are woody perennials; if they shed their leaves at the end of each growing season they are termed deciduous. Everything else you'll pick up as you go along. By the way, botanical Latin – like what it is spoke proper – has classical scholars wetting themselves with laughter, so don't be the least bit embarrassed about (mis)pronouncing plant names. Just give them your best shot like the rest of us.

Now that we're speaking the same language, how best to combine your plants? First and foremost, it's *your* garden, so it's *your* taste that counts. Using common sense as your guide, you'll be surprised how quickly everything falls into place after making only one opening move. The choice of a single plant sets the mind running after a suitable partner, then after a partner for that partner, and the process suddenly snowballs. Let's say a particular tall-growing perennial tickles your fancy. It could go next to a mature shrub. If the shrub is deciduous and the perennial is herbaceous, you'll feel the need of an evergreen in the vicinity. If they all

left: *Cornus alba* 'Sibirica'

flower in the same season, you'll want to introduce plants that bloom at other times in the year. You'll tend to put progressively shorter plants in front of the ones behind; you'll aim for contrast in the size, shape and texture of foliage; you'll concentrate on colour combinations you find especially pleasing. To close unsightly gaps, you'll learn to use annuals and biennials as temporary fillers while perennials grow to maturity. As space runs out, you'll learn to plant in layers, growing bulbs through ground-cover plants, shade-lovers under shrubs, and climbers through everything. You'll find plenty of suggestions in the text: more importantly, you'll soon have the confidence and knowledge to make connections of your own.

The great joy of a well-planted garden is that it simply gets better and better with age. Some subjects will roar away beyond your wildest expectations, others will quietly prosper. Guide their progress by tending regularly to their needs in an informed and leisurely fashion. A sensible pruning regime will keep your shrubs to the desired size and stimulate growth to new shoots, leaves and flowers. Annual applications of compost and manure to the soil will keep it weed-free, moist and well nourished. Lifting and dividing clumps of perennials before they become tired and congested will keep them eternally young and beautiful. Perpetuate short-lived shrubs and perennials by taking cuttings, so death never comes as a blow. Cultivate seedlings of annuals and biennials for a steady stream of replacements. Give your surpluses away to novices out of sheer generosity and to experienced gardeners out of enlightened self-interest. Who knows what treasures might come back in return?

Some people will have you believe that gardening is an art. This, I'm inclined to think, is rather uppity. Others insist it is a science. Much too cold and intimidating. Unquestionably the most helpful way to approach gardening is to regard it as a craft: you don't need divine inspiration, nor do you need a brain the size of a planet, all that is necessary is the will to succeed and a little application. As a process, gardening is mentally absorbing and physically invigorating. The end result is something truly magical and spiritually uplifting. The artist, remember, is Nature – and if the following pages teach you nothing else but to work with, not against, the prevailing conditions in your garden, then I'll consider my job done.

above: *Sarcococca hookeriana*

'If it is herein stated that roses will not grow like houseleeks on tiled roofs, nor

rhododendrons in beds of chalk, those points must be considered settled, for they do not

admit of discussion. But when it is further added that beds of roses do not assort tastefully

with geraniums, that coniferous trees are out of place in a flower border, there is room for

difference of opinion, and the reader is at liberty to quarrel with the author to any extent.'

James Shirley Hibberd (1825–1890)

winter

Ignore winter and you kiss a quarter of your gardening life goodbye. While most plants sleep, others dance to the rhythm of a different drum: flame-stemmed dogwoods shimmer over snowdrops, witch hazel and honeysuckle scent the frosty air, violet irises bloom and inviolate cherries blossom. Seize the day!

left: *Stachyurus chinensis*; above: *Helleborus foetidus*

adonis amurensis

Amur Adonis Named for the handsome toy boy of both Aphrodite, goddess of beauty, sexual love and fertility, and Persephone, Queen of the Underworld, the adonis is a darn fine thing, yes, ma'am. Not just a pretty face but fully hardy too, it was introduced to the West in 1896 from its natural habitat on mountainous north- and east-facing woodland slopes in Manchuria where the river Amur marks the border with Siberia.

An aristocratic member of the ranunculus family, it is taller, more distinguished and earlier to flower than the European spring adonis (*Adonis vernalis*), though later to rise – naturally – than their yeoman cousin the winter aconite (*Eranthis hyemalis*). Its glistening 6cm/2½in 20- to 50-petalled buttercup yellow blooms are borne aloft on initially short stems, which soon attain a height of 20cm/8in or so. While Adonis was a short-lived beauty gored to death in his prime, his flowers last a good six weeks unless nipped by frost.

Cultivated varieties include the wide open, early semi-double 'Fukujukai' and the doubles 'Flore Pleno', which is yellow with a green cast, and 'Pleniflora', with sulphur petals surrounding a prominent (if not downright peculiar) green eye. 'Hinomotu' is a vibrant orange-red and Japanese nurserymen, who have very much taken this plant to heart, have also developed much sought-after pink and white forms.

In late winter established clumps resemble a florist's dream crop of ready-made gentlemen's buttonholes, since each bare-stemmed bloom wears a ruff-like collar of feathery leaves. Ferny, finely cut and a fetching shade of apple green, the foliage proper follows swiftly behind and is attractive in its own right. It reaches a height of 30–45cm/12–18in by mid summer at which point it promptly disappears as the plant goes dormant. Just as Zeus decreed for Adonis himself, it spends half the year with us and Aphrodite, the rest with Persephone in Hades.

It is tempting to associate colonies of adonis with winter irises and crocuses for a vibrant shot of early colour, but in the garden this approach leads to whacking great summertime gaps. Opt instead for the late emerging purple-blue balloon flower, *Platycodon grandiflorus*, or for a stylish Japanese-inspired foliage contrast, you'll find hostas make ideal planting companions.

Soil and site The Amur adonis thrives on moist, acid, humus-rich soils and requires a good six hours a day of winter sunshine to bloom, yet relishes summer shade. Simply replicate its home surroundings by planting beneath deciduous trees or shrubs. Note that these are quite the opposite conditions required by the spring adonis and the winter aconite, which prefer well-drained alkaline soil in full sun. On any given site you can only grow one lot successfully.

Care and propagation The *Adonis amurensis* is hearty and robust but takes a little time to bed down comfortably after planting and resents subsequent disturbance. However, should congestion noticeably affect performance then lift and divide old clumps as the leaves are fading. Tenderly separate the massed, cord-like roots and replant at the same depth, taking the opportunity to enrich the planting holes with leaf-mould or well-rotted garden compost.

left: *A. a.* 'Fukujukai'

arum italicum subsp. italicum 'marmoratum'

Italian arum Before I'm accused of writing with a stutter a little botany is in order. Plants are categorized by family then named by genus, by species and finally by variety or cultivar. The Araceae family encompasses well over a hundred weird and wonderful genera from *Arisaema* to *Zantedeschia*, which divide into more than two thousand species, including that ubiquitous houseplant yet rare rainforest native, the Swiss cheese plant (*Monstera deliciosa*) and the mouse plant (*Arisarum proboscideum*), a common southern European wildflower that remains a garden novelty. Now, *Arum italicum* is such a variable species it has been split into four subspecies. The one to catch every gardener's fancy is subsp. *italicum* whose beautifully cream veined and marbled leaves reach their apogee in 'Marmoratum'. Phew! Gardeners are more pragmatic than taxonomists, so *A. italicum* 'Marmoratum' generally does the trick on a shopping list, as does its old name 'Pictum', which was dropped to avoid confusion with *A. pictum* – but enough already.

Whatever the weather, every autumn elegant spear-shaped leaves unfurl from tightly rolled snouts sent up by the fat tuberous roots. If they're nipped by early frosts new shoots soon replace them. Older foliage is remarkably resilient: ice can turn it limp as a vicar's handshake but a thaw soon has it standing back to attention. Leaves up to 30cm/12in long on leaf-stalks (petioles) of equal length are not uncommon, so the size and dignity of these plants alone would make them valuable additions to the winter garden; with their dramatic variegation they're indispensable. But there's even more...

The late spring lords and ladies type flowers pass unnoticed by all but pollinating flies who find them warm (really – it's a chemical reaction), smelly (secretions, don't you know) and scrumptious (oh dear). When the leaves melt away as summer looms, having replenished the tubers' food reserves, the plant is easily forgotten. The club-like fruiting spikes only draw attention to themselves in early autumn when, by ripening from green to scarlet they appear as if by magic amongst the fading leaves of summer blooming perennials. If the birds aren't too peckish the tightly packed stems of berries hang around to complement the new season's foliage and make a truly heart-warming early winter scene.

Awkward sites Hard to plant areas of dry shade are mother's milk to Italian arums. Native to south and west Europe and North Africa too, they thrive under hedges and in stony soil up against walls. Clumps in sunnier spots require richer, moister soil but reward you with more pronounced marbling to the leaves. Unnaturally lush conditions provide spectacular leaves prone to attack from slugs and flower arrangers, otherwise the plants are long-lived and pest-free. Work the same site twice as hard by interplanting herbaceous geraniums like *Geranium himalayense* 'Gravetye' or *G. macrorrhizum*, which send up foliage in spring, flower in summer, then colour and die back in autumn.

Propagation With the help of birds, seedlings can pop up anywhere but the variegation takes two years to show so bide your time before weeding out duller specimens. Particularly fine examples can be perpetuated when mature either by lifting and dividing the roots in late summer or by removing and replanting offsets arising from the parent tuber.

asplenium scolopendrium

Made for shade Full or heavily dappled shade is all the robust hart's tongue fern needs to flourish. Ordinary garden soil is quite rich enough and provides ample moisture but enrich poor soils with compost or leaf mould and add humus and grit to heavy soils to open up the texture and improve drainage. Acid soil is fine but alkaline conditions are preferred. Clay will be tolerated just so long as it doesn't waterlog in winter.

These amiable ferns are a boon for problem places where little else will grow. Try them in the shadiest nooks of banks and rockeries – the sloping ground guards against winter wet. Bog plants thrive on the margins of natural pools but not around ponds lined with butyl or concrete where the soil is in fact dry; in moderate shade, hart's tongues make a luxuriant and visually appropriate substitute – their roots are happy and the fronds are more sun-tolerant in a humid atmosphere. They also work well in the dappled light beneath the slats of garden benches, in planting pockets in retaining walls and at the foot of buildings and hedges. To make an attractive year-round feature of an old tree stump, plant it up with a mixture of these ferns and yellow-leaved ivy *Hedera helix* 'Buttercup'.the beautiful

Coughs and sneezes Too much sunlight gives the fronds jaundice; serious sunburn results in nasty brown scars. A fungal rust will arise in damp conditions and presents symptoms similar to sunburn with the addition of chalky spores in the middle of the lesions on the underside of fronds. If sun is the problem move plants somewhere shadier. If dank and damp are to blame then move them somewhere drier and airier after removing all affected leaves. The safest time for transplanting is in early spring before new leaves emerge.

Propagation Growing ferns from spores is tedious, time-consuming and best left to professionals or bores. Good garden forms are sterile anyway so you'd be on a hiding to nothing if you tried. Colonies can be divided but I think it's a shame to disturb them; if you want more plants, buy something new to extend your collection.

> Many suitable positions for hardy ferns may be found in most gardens where their culture is not now attempted. **George Nicholson (1847–1908)**

Hart's tongue fern All ferns like boggy conditions. True or false? It's false! This common misconception has led to such serious abuse and neglect that countless varieties have been lost to cultivation since their Victorian heyday when ferns were all the rage both indoors and out. Nowadays people with dry soil dismiss them out of hand and those with damp patches kill them off in record time. It's all gone topsy-turvy.

Never make connections where none exist. Just as bad musicians confuse tempo and volume, slowing down while playing *pianissimo* then speeding up for *forte*, so naive gardeners automatically equate a plant's love of shade with a need for damp. For most ferns this simply isn't the case. In fact, for many, including the otherwise indestructible hart's tongue, wet feet prove fatal.

Native to Britain and mainland Europe, *Asplenium scolopendrium* forms irregular shuttlecock-like crowns of strappy fronds 30–60cm/12–24in long that are always smooth and glossy with a prominent central vein, then gently ruched or extravagantly ruffled and crested according to variety. The appeal is that of an attractive man in a crumpled dinner-jacket: smart, dandified and louche, all at the same time. You'll soon be seduced.

When choosing and combining cultivars, aim for contrast and exercise restraint. The Crispum Group offers deeply goffered fronds and *A. s.* 'Crispum Bolton's Nobile' is arguably the pick of the bunch. Those in the Cristatum Group have a cockscomb tip; the Marginatum Group, lobed and shredded edges. Plants in the Ramocristatum Group have fronds that split fan-like at the base, with each branch crested (think lollo rosso); those in the Ramomarginatum Group have lobed fronds that branch repeatedly along their length (think curly endive). The ideal hart's tongue planting is a simple mix of a few sophisticated leaves.

Up against a wall or in the shrubbery?
Confusion with its relatives has given *Azara microphylla* an undeserved reputation as a tender wee soul when in fact it's reliably hardy in all but the coldest areas. On home ground it favours woodland margins so sun is less important than shelter. It makes an ideal wall shrub in light shade, but the cooler your climate the more it will appreciate either the reflected heat from a sunny garden wall in summer (to ripen young wood against the onslaught of frost) or the radiant warmth of a house wall in winter. Protect young specimens from cold winds in the open garden by making them part of a mixed shrub planting. In maturity they form large shrubs or small trees according to your pruning. Happy in any soil, *A. microphylla* is pest and trouble free.
Pruning For wall-grown specimens trim off outward growing shoots after flowering. To form a tree progressively remove lower side shoots as the main stem develops over the years. Otherwise leave well alone except to remove dead or awkwardly growing shoots.

azara microphylla

Azara Of the ten or so species in this genus of evergreen flowering shrubs and trees from Chile and Argentina *Azara microphylla*, being the hardiest, is the first one a gardener should plump for. Besides making the garden smell like a French patisserie its flowers are followed in hot summers by large quantities of petite orange-red berries, while the curious arrangement of tiny leaves makes it an intriguing background foliage shrub all year round.

Closely packed parallel rows of stems run at a slant down either side of the branches like herring bones and the glossy oval deep green leaves run in similar fashion down these side stems. The odd thing is that each one comes with its own mini-me, a quarter-sized replica jutting out at an angle where the real leaf meets the stem. Botanically these are stipules, the best-known garden examples being the little green scale we take for granted at the base of a rose's leaf-stalk and the pair of miniature leaves on the flower stem a little below each rose bloom. The azara's

prominent stipules overlap each other slightly to give a lacy, plaited effect which, while not exactly dramatic, is charming close-up and lends distinct textural interest at a distance. If you can track one down, this effect is highlighted very prettily by the creamy leaf-margins of the notoriously slow growing *A. m.* 'Variegata'.

Plants are always in bloom by late winter and earlier still in mild years and protected locations. The flowers have no petals, so withstand cold well, and are simply clusters of stamens (the male flower organs) atop prominent ovaries. These little yellow tassels are borne in small groups between the leaves on the underside of the twigs and they rely on their amazing vanilla fragrance to attract pollinators. Later-blooming species are built to a larger scale with more prominent mimosa-like flower pom-poms, but they are rather tender and so for adventurous or warm-climate gardeners only. Frost damage is unmistakable, the leaves turn black almost instantly! *A. integrifolia*, *A. lanceolata* and *A. petiolaris* start flowering in spring, *A. dentata* saves itself for summer.

Optimum conditions Bergenias grown in moist humus-rich soil and given some shade from hot afternoon sun will amaze your friends and mystify your enemies.

Propagation Lift and divide old clumps after flowering in spring. Alternatively cut or snap off lengths of rhizome in autumn to plant where you fancy.

Problems Slugs and snails often take refuge in the cool shade of the leaves then go on night-time safari for daintier morsels. Pick them off by day to keep the rest of your garden intact.

Spoilt for choice *Bergenia cordifolia* 'Purpurea' has magenta-purple flowers and leaves that colour well. *B. crassifolia* 'Aureo-Marginata' has leaves variegated cream and purple-green. *B.* x *schmidtii* is sturdy and vigorous. *B.* 'Ballawley' is extremely large and colours well but its leaves are thinner than usual and sometimes sustain frost damage.

bergenia purpurascens

Elephant's ears · pigsqueaks Bergenias have impeccable credentials. From the Altai Mountains they reached the west in 1765 via the Empress of Russia and Carl Linnaeus, father of modern botany. Their huge round leaves were all the rage in Victorian gardens and flower arrangements, and Gertrude Jekyll (rhymes with treacle), doyenne of twentieth-century gardening, used them extensively and praised them repeatedly.

These hardy, vigorous and extremely obliging evergreen perennials are excellent ground cover for any soil or situation, even dry shade under trees. But quiet, helpful children aren't always given the attention they deserve, and gardeners too rarely provide bergenias with optimum growing conditions.

Bergenia cordifolia has almost circular heart-shaped leaves that are leathery in texture and have a wavy outline. They grow to 20cm/8in across on thick leaf-stalks. These arise directly from fleshy stems called rhizomes which creep horizontally just below ground, rooting as they go to form broad, dense clumps 30cm/12in in height. Tight bunches of a dozen or so individual rose-pink flowers appear from late winter to early spring and are held just a little above the leaves.

On *B. crassifolia*, each oval leaf-blade tails away down the petiole, so the foliage is essentially spoon shaped. The leaves are smaller and shinier than *B. cordifolia* but at 50cm/20in or so, the loosely branched flower stalks are much taller with panicles of lilac-pink spring blooms held in loose sprays.

The flowers are a bonus. What makes bergenias so essential to the winter garden is the rich cast of polished mahogany to deep maroon assumed by the leaves at the onset of cold weather. This warm welcoming glow remains until spring when the foliage reverts to dark green. Literally as tough as old boots, the leaves' unusually high tannin content has been used for both dye and anti-freeze; in Kashmir the rhizomes are a substitute for tea.

For superlative colour opt for the dainty *B. purpurascens*, a Himalayan native with paddle-shaped leaves that are purple-brown in summer and beetroot red in winter. Its magenta or shocking pink flowers complement the foliage well and are a mid to late spring treat. Though a truly outstanding garden plant it is less vigorous than the two more commonly grown species and won't tolerate poor or dry soil to anything like the same extent. Cherish it.

chimonanthus praecox

Wintersweet · *La-Mei* (Chinese) · *Obai* (Japanese)

In the Chinese floral calendar wintersweet represents *La*, the twelfth lunar month, and can always be relied upon to flower in the dead of the cold season. Branches of this woodland shrub's spicily fragrant blooms had long been used as decorations for the Chinese New Year before plants were domesticated during the Sung dynasty (960–1126AD) in response to a poem by Huang Tingjian. In 1766 a specimen was sent to the Earl of Coventry at Croome in Worcestershire where it was planted (quite unnecessarily) in the conservatory. New introductions are invariably overprotected and mollycoddled but wintersweet was soon recognised as fully hardy and straightforward to grow. By 1838, according to John Claudius Loudon, it was 'grown in most choice gardens for its flowers, a few of which are gathered daily and placed in the drawing room or boudoir, in the same manner as violets'. Indoors and out, the haunting violet, jonquil and cinnamon scent penetrates the air for yards around. Even the wood is stunningly aromatic, so cut any prunings into short lengths then tie them in small bundles for scenting drawers and clothes cupboards.

Wintersweet's beautifully translucent cup-shaped lemon-yellow flowers reach 2.5cm/1in across and have purple-stained centres. They generously cloak the bare stems throughout the second half of winter well in advance of the 7–16cm/3–6in leaves, which appear in spring. Pendent in habit and with finger-like waxy petals, the flowers are incredibly well designed to repel lashing snow and rain and can withstand all but the most severe frost. Straightforward *Chimonanthus praecox* is far and away the most heavily fragrant form but if you buy your scent for the bottle *C. p.* 'Grandiflorus' has significantly larger blooms while those of *C. p.* var. *luteus* open wider but later and are bright golden yellow all over.

Prune lightly Prune wintersweet after flowering only to maintain shape or to train plants against a sunny wall, where they will bloom earlier and more abundantly.

Patience is a virtue Flowers only appear on well-ripened mature wood so don't expect anything from a young specimen until it has had at least three or four years to gear up.

Good companions Once the leaves supersede the flowers, wintersweet is an anonymous-looking shrub of open habit. For maximum year-round impact run a fast-growing climber or two through it. Herbaceous specimens like the annual *Ipomoea* 'Heavenly Blue' (p.98) or the perennial *Lathyrus grandiflorus* (p.99) are both prolific summer bloomers that can be cut down and disentangled come leaf-fall. Most woody climbers are out of the question because their straggly stems would be distracting in winter. However, clematis in the Viticella Group extend the season brilliantly because they flower from mid summer to early autumn then require hard pruning to just a bud or two above ground level as winter approaches. Try 'Blue Belle', which has well-rounded violet blue flowers to 9cm/3¹/₂in across, or the dark purple cross-like flowers of 'Polish Spirit'.

Planting This clematis requires rich but well-drained soil and resents winter wetness. Many clematis are planted deeply to guard against wilt but this one should simply be potted out in the ordinary way with the top of its root ball level with the surrounding soil. All clematis roots like a certain amount of summer shade. Misguided souls use slates or stone slabs. Don't! They create hidey-holes for slugs, snails and woodlice. It is far better to plant a spreading, low-growing shrub or perennial nearby.

No pruning required However, to stop well-established plants outgrowing their allocated space (they can spread to well over 6m/20ft) you may wish to cut them back annually, once flowering is over, to 1m/3ft from the ground.

Go wild Plant this clematis up trellises, fences and walls by all means, but for a lovely natural look let it scramble over large shrubs or informal hedges that don't require too much pruning. *Rosa moyesii* (p.144) and *Rosa rugosa* are not only accommodating hosts, but they flower in summer and fruit in autumn so the combination looks stunning all year round.

clematis cirrhosa var. balearica

Fern-leaved clematis The creamy white 4cm/1½in bell-shaped flowers of this mid winter to early spring blooming climber are prettily speckled maroon and somewhat resemble hellebores. No prizes for guessing what the evergreen leaves look like. This attractive package of flowers and foliage has many charms. The nodding blooms are lemon-scented and tend to turn pink with age. Their massed stamens add considerably to the decorative effect, consisting of long, palest green filaments tipped with large yellow pollen-bearing anthers. The shiny leaves are flushed bronze-purple round their toothed margins and take on more colour with the advent of winter when their matt undersides can appear dark red.

As you might expect of a plant native to the Balearic Islands in the western Mediterranean, the fern-leaved clematis is not fully hardy but it is certainly frost hardy to -5°C/23°F and well worth trying in all but the very coldest of climates. As is ever the case in the winter garden, a warm sheltered spot, perhaps against

a wall, helps any plant resist the worst your weather can throw at it. You can even grow this versatile clematis in a cool conservatory, which will extend its flowering season from mid autumn to spring.

With its good looks and vigorous constitution *Clematis cirrhosa* var. *balearica* is undoubtedly the best example for average conditions. For warmer gardens and for conservatories it is well worth considering a form of the north Algerian *C. c.* var. *purpurascens* known as 'Freckles'. Flowering from late autumn to mid winter this has large petals that are so heavily spotted inside as to be almost totally rose-maroon, a stunning contrast to their creamy exteriors. Each bloom is as luscious as a peeled ripe fig, quartered and squeezed open ready to eat.

Whichever variety you choose, the attractive seedheads are a knockout in spring – every stem is covered in starbursts of silken tassels that ripen to fluffy puffs of snow.

cornus alba 'sibirica'

Westonbirt dogwood Stems, if they are thought about at all, are looked upon as clothes horses for leaves and flowers. Only very rarely are they sufficiently attractive to hold our eye in their own right. The American dewy willow, *Salix irrorata*, has dark purple stems dusted with the white powdery bloom usually associated with ripe plums and black grapes. The Japanese wineberry, *Rubus phoenicolasius*, is so densely covered with many thousands of fine, hairy thorns that its reddish brown stems look oddly out of focus. The Mount Omei rose *Rosa sericea* subsp. *omeiensis* f. *pteracantha* has such extraordinarily large translucent red thorns they virtually defy belief. Winter, of course, is the perfect time to admire them in their full naked glory.

The most gobsmacking stems of all belong to the Westonbirt dogwood. They are bright coral or sealing wax red and grow whippy and upright in dense flame-effect thickets, which rarely exceed 1m/3ft in gardens because of their harsh but simple pruning regime. Incredibly hardy and happy on any soil, rich or poor, dry or wet, *Cornus alba* 'Sibirica' will illuminate any winter scene, although a site in full summer sun produces the most brilliant stems of all. They spread rampantly alongside water and are truly spectacular when reflected in pools or streams.

Flat clusters of flowers appear in late spring and early summer. They are followed towards the close of summer by the white, sometimes blue-tinged berries (perversely) referred to in the specific name *alba* (the plant's red, red, I tell you!). The dark green spear-shaped leaves are up to 10cm/4in long and colour orange, red and purple in autumn. For optimum year-round impact plant *C. a.* 'Sibirica Variegata' whose foliage has slapdash but generous white margins and attractive, randomly placed central patches of light grey-green. If you are planting several specimens together, it looks devilish mixed with the yellow-stemmed *C. stolonifera* 'Flaviramea'.

Coppicing The youngest wood is the brightest and shiniest; old stems become thick, coarse and dull. This rather brutal technique promotes a continuous annual supply of handsome new growth. Because it is so simple and so rewarding it also gives hesitant gardeners the confidence to tackle more sophisticated pruning jobs as they arise. Just cut everything to within a few inches of the ground in early spring. If the sudden gap shocks you, approach the task on a rolling basis: remove two-year-old stems annually but leave the one-year-olds alone. The result is a larger, looser shrub with a beguiling two-tone winter effect.

Go for it The rounded leaves of the smoke bush *Cotinus coggygria* 'Royal Purple' contrast beautifully with those of *Cornus alba* 'Sibirica Variegata'. To keep this large bushy tree in proportion (and to produce outsized foliage)... you guessed right, coppice the brute from an early age.

left: *Cornus stolonifera* 'Flaviramea';
C. alba 'Sibirica'

corylus avellana 'contorta'

Contorted hazel · Corkscrew hazel · Harry Lauder's walking stick A vigorous grower, hazel produces branches so often and from so low down it is more of a shrub than a tree. Happy in any soil, it can handle heavy shade or full sun. In medieval England it was used for everything from wattle-and-daub house walls, thatching spars and fences to basket-work, kindling and firewood. Extensive copses were planted and one seventh of the wood was harvested each year so there was a rolling supply of poles in a dependable range of length and thickness. Modern fuels and materials have long since supplanted hazel as an economic commodity, but it is still highly valued in gardens, especially because of the contorted form found in Gloucestershire in 1863. Like Josephine Baker at her outrageous best, its handsome limbs dance and writhe with *joie de vivre*.

This loopiness extends to the rough, broad-toothed mid-green leaves, which are distinctly puckered. In autumn they turn yellow before falling to reveal the lengthening buds of the male catkins. By mid winter, dusty golden lambs' tails dangle seductively in the wind; their soft, serried verticals contrast beautifully with the lithe, dark brown stems. Silhouetted against a plain background, or better still the sky, the corkscrew hazel is a plant to die for.

Think hazel and you think nuts. Though orchard strains like the 'Emperor Cob' or 'Webb's Prize Cob' bear well, don't expect too many nuts from *Corylus avellana* 'Contorta', they are as rare as hens' teeth. For interest's sake though, look out for the tiny female catkins in spring. Apart from a star-like tuft of red stigmas – the sticky receptive flower parts – they resemble leaf buds and are easily overlooked. Hazels don't put out foliage until mid to late spring, the better for winter winds to blow copious amounts of pollen unimpeded through their woodland habitat until all passion is spent. Such wantonness gives us all the more time to admire their naked limbs.

Pruning in a nutshell The stems develop more character with age, so don't prune until you have to. Improve an established plant's overall appearance with the odd cosmetic snip in late winter to reduce congested top growth. Use secateurs or a sharp knife to make clean cuts just above an incipient leaf bud. New woody growth will spring from this node, so make sure it is outward-facing. Keep older specimens shapely and within bounds by trimming back more drastically. Every few years, it helps to saw an old stem back almost to the ground to keep the habit light and airy.

Propagate by layering Cuttings don't take well but small rooted shoots at the base of the plants can sometimes be detached and potted up for growing on. Otherwise, select a whippy low-growing stem and nick the bark below a leaf node on the underside to stimulate root formation. Peg this part down into the soil and in a year or two's time you'll have a man-made rooted shoot. This procedure is known as layering.

Trimming Left unpruned, hawthorns form large shrubs or small trees. If young specimens are planted 30–35cm/12–14in apart and trimmed annually they form smart, dense hedges. *Crataegus monogyna* is an especially suitable candidate as it has a strong tendency to branch right from the base. Clip it with shears after flowering in spring or, for more berries, wait until late autumn.

Wildlife The berries attract birds in winter and well-established plants offer secure nesting sites in spring. With a bit of luck, the adults will fatten their fledglings on insects from your vegetable patch. A diversity of wildlife is the key to a well-balanced, pest-free garden.

Fireblight This disease causes leaves and stems to wither and die. It enters via open flowers and can kill a plant within a few years unless affected branches are pruned well back to healthy wood. It is less likely to make headway if plants are trimmed in spring. Sorry, birdies.

crataegus monogyna 'biflora'

Glastonbury thorn The genus *Crataegus* or hawthorn, has about two hundred species spread liberally throughout North America and northern Europe with perhaps a thousand naturally occurring varieties, garden cultivars and hybrids (crosses between species). The choice for gardeners is breathtaking.

Hawthorns have a long season of interest and their extreme hardiness is valuable in coastal and exposed gardens where they make attractive windbreaks. Making a better ornamental hedge than many shrubs, they quickly form an impenetrable barrier of steely, criss-crossing twigs ferociously armed with long spiny thorns that are needle-sharp. Forget barbed wire! In late spring they are so smothered with large flat-topped corymbs or bunches of frothy blossom that you can barely see the lobed, diamond-shaped leaves. These corymbs are laden in autumn with berries resembling tiny apples or rosehips and the foliage of some species colours well before falling. *Crataegus laevigata* 'Punicea' has scarlet blossom and deep red fruits while *C. l.* 'Rosea Flore Pleno' has double pink flowers. *C. mollis* (red haw) has white flowers and large showy fruit hanging in clusters like cherries.

C. x lavalleei 'Carrierei' has white flowers with pink anthers and long dark green leaves that accompany its orange-red berries long into winter.

And speaking of winter…The English hawthorn *C. monogyna* is a charming enough sight in hedgerows but 'Biflora' is altogether magical and has acquired a wealth of folklore. The most popular legend has Joseph of Arimathea arriving through snow from the Holy Land to build a church in Glastonbury. To persuade the doubting townspeople of his mission he prayed for a miracle then struck his staff into the ground where it immediately took root and blossomed. The staff itself is sometimes said to have grown from the crown of thorns, the autumn berries evoking the blood of Christ. What is without doubt is that its white blossom appears first in mid winter and then again at the normal time in spring. Although the precocious flowers are not to be relied on in exceptionally cold winters, they appear regularly in mild seasons or in sheltered locations. Miraculous or not, these give the Glastonbury thorn an edge over all others when selecting a form for your garden.

cyclamen coum

Choices, choices Orchid-like *C. c. f. albissimum* has white reflexed petals with a carmine-red mouth to each flower and characteristic dark green kidney-shaped leaves. *C. c.* subsp. *caucasicum* has pinkish lilac blooms and scalloped leaves with lustrous silver-grey markings. The Pewter Group has leaves that are almost entirely silvered above but still reddish or green and red beneath: 'Maurice Dryden' has pure white blooms; 'Tilebarn Elizabeth' is outstanding with pale pink flowers that colour more deeply at the petal tips and have full, dark lips.

Propagation After pollination the peduncle, or flower stalk, coils flat to the ground like a watchspring. *Cyclamen* comes from the Greek *kyklos*, meaning circular, which refers to this spiralling action. Seeds ripen the summer after flowering and germinate readily in the soil around the parent plant. For a more widespread distribution collect seeds from the capsules as they begin to split and poke them into the earth where you want them to grow. Seedlings take three years to flower.

When is a bulb not a bulb? 'Bulb' is used as a loose generic term. Strictly, a bulb consists of swollen leaf bases. A corm is a swollen stem base. A tuber is a fleshy stem or root, and a rhizome is a thick horizontally running stem. All can be used for the storage of food during a resting season. And a weasel is weasily recognized but a stoat is stoatally different.

left: *Cyclamen coum* right: *C. c.* 'Album'

Sowbread There's no mistaking the elegant shuttlecock flowers of cyclamen. Florists sell them as houseplants by the barrowload in all shades from bright crimson and mauve to the common pale pink then on to purest white. These cultivars are the results of generations of careful breeding and selection from *Cyclamen persicum*. They are mass-produced for our delectation in state-of-the-art, factory-sized glass-houses. They generally start to ail from the moment of purchase and only with exceptional care can we persuade them to flower even half as well for us the following year. Let's not even mention poinsettias.

It is with a sense of awe and disbelief then that novice gardeners first see sheets of miniature cyclamen growing happily outdoors in the middle of winter and early in spring. How on earth is it possible? Well, you just plant a few tubers of hardy *C. coum* then leave them well alone.

Young tubers are about 3cm/1¼in in diameter with a flattened or concave upper surface and should only be buried about 2.5–5cm/1–2in deep. Because each leaf and flower grows on a separate stem from the top of the bulb, the remains of these stalks can be mistaken for roots, with the result that the bulbs are sometimes planted upside down. To avoid this, all you have to remember is that the top looks a bit like a ring doughnut while the base looks more like a jam doughnut. If you're still undecided then hold off planting until the roots are just showing.

The tubers dry out quickly so plant them as soon after purchase as possible. A counsel of perfection would be to buy them fat and plump just before coming out of dormancy in late summer and early autumn. The most foolproof method of all is to plant out 'in the green' from pot-bought specimens but this can prove very expensive.

Wild *C. coum* inhabit rocky, wooded terrain in semi-arid locations from Bulgaria and Turkey to the Caucasus, Lebanon and Israel. In gardens they go where no plant has gone before, right into root-riddled soil in the shade of deciduous trees and shrubs. Dry soil or good drainage are essential if the tubers are not to fall prey to rot. Large surrounding root systems absorb excess moisture in spring and summer while gritty, leaf-rich soil aids drainage in autumn and winter. Give them a light sprinkling of bonemeal after flowering to provide a welcome nutrient boost for next season's growth.

daphne mezereum

Mezereon Though a master of minute observation Hanmer, as befitted a gentleman, was prone to understatement. The mauve-pink to purple-red flowers of this long-standing cottage garden favourite are more than a little sweet: they blast the air with a saccharine-sharp fragrance cut by the bitterness of plum kernels. Outdoors the scent is intoxicating, indoors it is head-achingly keen. Bear this in mind if you're tempted to use mezereon stems as cut flowers. If your scissor fingers are still twitching, there are two more things you should know. All parts of the plant contain the poisonous irritant mezerein – according to Linnaeus, six berries will kill a wolf – so take care not to get sap on your hands. For their part daphnes, which are short-lived

at the best of times, are especially prone to dieback caused by fungal spores entering through cuts and wounds. You don't want to hasten their demise. Or yours.

There's always space for a mezereon. Rarely exceeding 1m/3ft this is a particularly valuable and attractive shrub for small gardens. In late winter the stemless flowers form long shish-kebabs of colour on wood grown the previous summer. They remain a feature until well into spring when fresh leaves sprout pineapple-fashion at the top of the blooms as the new season's woody growth begins. The berries ripen to scarlet in mid summer. White flowering forms bear amber yellow fruit. Birds scarf them down but wolves won't touch them. Children should follow the latter example.

> The flowers have but four very small leaves [petals] apiece, and break forth of the very wood of the branches as those of the Judas tree doe, before the greene leaves appeare. They are a little sweet, and turne into berryes...

Thomas Hanmer (1612–1678)

Soil and site The mezereon enjoys a rich loamy soil that is moist but free-draining. Acid or alkaline conditions suit it equally well. A native of European and Asian woodlands, it prefers light shade but will tolerate full sun.
Pruning Swiftly remove any damaged or diseased wood. The only other justification for using your secateurs is to take cuttings.
Semi-ripe cuttings Self-sown seedlings are common but they won't necessarily have such good flower colour as their parents. Layering is the best way to perpetuate a good strain but you can also strike cuttings. In late summer remove the year's new growth from a stem and trim the base to just below a leaf node. Shorten the cutting to 12cm/5in or so by snipping just above a node. Remove any leaves from the lower half then plunge it to its middle into a pot of soil, firming well. Put the pot in a shady place and keep the soil barely moist. In two or three years you'll have a garden-ready plant.

left: *Daphne mezereum* var. *rubra*

erica carnea

Routine care Heathers like soils that are rich in humus so mix a lot of peat, leafmould or garden compost into planting holes. Coming from moorland and mountain habitats they like nothing better than a bracing, windswept site. Heathers can grow lank and leggy but *E. carnea* and its hybrids have a tight growth habit and need little maintenance. When the bells fade, clip them with shears to just below the old flowering portion of the stem. New leaf growth is often creamy-green at first and can be an attractive spring feature in its own right. The simplest way to propagate named forms is to tug small, rooted shoots away from large, well-established plants.

Don't go there Kidney-shaped beds spotted with heathers and dwarf conifers are a nightmare of the Seventies. Cast them from your mind. Use *E. carnea* and *E.* x *darleyensis* sparingly wherever you want a splash of winter colour and a pool of summer greenery.

Alpine heath · winter heath If you thought your soil wouldn't grow heathers, it will. If you think you don't like them, take a second look.

Heathers were not grown as garden plants until the mid-eighteenth century when it became common practice to collect attractive seedlings from moorlands. *Erica carnea*, a central and southern European native, was brought into cultivation by the ever accumulative George William, Earl of Coventry, in 1763 and proved a great success. It is 20–25cm/8–10in tall and bears urn-shaped purple-pink flowers reliably from early winter to early spring. Most important of all, it doesn't throw hysterics at a touch of lime. Heathers will normally only grow in acid conditions, the Alpine heath thrives in any garden soil. It shares this useful characteristic with one other species, *E. erigena*, the extraordinarily beautiful Irish heath. This attains a massive 2.5m/8ft, can be used for loose hedges, and carries honey-scented, lilac-pink flowers in profusion from late winter into late spring. Unfortunately, its tall brittle stems often break under the weight of snow and, unlike its cousin, it is not reliably hardy so it is less common in gardens. But wait for it...

As the eighteenth century drew to a close a chance seedling, which was a hybrid of the two species, arose in a nursery in Darley Dale in Derbyshire. *E.* x *darleyensis* is hardy, fragrant, bears masses of flowers and has a longer season than either of its parents. It is around the same size as *E. carnea*. Discerning selection from the wild and careful breeding programmes in nurseries have since produced many outstanding cultivars. In a warm year or on a favoured site many will bloom from as early as mid autumn.

E. carnea 'King George' is sturdy, thickly clustered with deep pink bells and blooms early in winter; *E. c.* 'Springwood White' is quick growing and bears pure brilliant white bells in long sprays suitable for cutting; *E. c.* 'Vivellii' has bronze leaves and mauve flowers that darken to magenta. *E.* x *darleyensis* 'Silberschmelze' is a neatly rounded plant carrying silver-white blooms from autumn to late spring; *E.* x *d.* 'Furzey' has strong spikes of dark rose purple; *E.* x *d* 'Ghost Hills' has short stems crowded with rose to red flowers, a first flush appears in autumn and is followed, after a lull, by a second flush in spring.

above: *Erica carnea* 'Golden Starlet'

galanthus

Snowdrop I can think of no more heart-warming and uplifting sight on a cold winter's day than a grassy wooded bank of gently nodding snowdrops. Like exquisite pieces of art nouveau jewellery, they command admiration not only for their intrinsic beauty but for the intricacy of their construction. Curled, glaucous green leaves surround each 10–15cm/4–6in flower stem which grows directly from the ground and is called a scape. At the top of each scape is a protective green spathe, or hood, which splits to reveal a solitary droplet-shaped bud on a slender stalk called a pedicel. So thin is this pedicel that the opening bloom hangs like a pendant earring on a wire loop.

The flowers are usually pure white (*Galanthus* comes from the Greek *gala*, milk, and *anthus*, flower) but can be marked green at the tips and throat. If you get down on your hands and knees you'll find they have an elusive honey fragrance with a mossy backnote and a faint metallic tang like the smell of plate glass. Bees are often to be seen gathering nectar on sunny winter days, pollinating as they go.

Seedlings take several years to flower, then after four years or so mature bulbs begin to produce offsets. Given ideal growing conditions, snowdrops will form large colonies and many apparently wild drifts in rough grass, on roadsides and at woodland edges have in fact spread from a few cultivated specimens planted many years earlier.

The most commonly seen snowdrop is *Galanthus nivalis* but there are about nineteen species in all and countless varieties and cultivars. For all their seeming innocence they're a promiscuous lot. By growing a range of them you can have a surprisingly long flowering season, and they might just breed some new varieties of their own.

Precocious *G. reginae-olgae* surprises everyone by flowering in autumn and goes against type by preferring a well-drained and sunny site. It has a translucent silvery line down the middle of each leaf as does *G. reginae-olgae* subsp. *vernalis* which blooms in late winter and early spring.

The highly variable *G. caucasicus* blooms from late autumn to early spring. Its short inner petals are tipped bright green.

Winter flowering *G. nivalis* has a double form called 'Flore Pleno' with a dense rosette of inner petals. Plants in the Scharlockii Group spread vigorously and have distinctive spathes which split to resemble donkey's ears; they are late blooming and the three long outer petals are green at the tips.

Buying and planting Snowdrops can either be planted as bulbs in autumn or 'in the green' once flowering is over in spring. Bury the bulbs three times as deep as they are round. The plumper they are, the better they establish; small dry bulbs are a waste of money. Specialist nurseries and good garden centres sell freshly lifted snowdrops bunched like spring onions or scallions. Gently divide them and plant each bulb individually to the depth it was grown at. Spread the roots loosely in a generous planting hole and completely cover the creamy-green leaf bases with soil, leaving only the dark green top growth on show. This can be a time-consuming operation so if you're lifting and dividing your own snowdrops, don't dig up more than you can handle. And don't take shortcuts with shallow planting, they'll just keel over and die.

Naturalizing in grass Use a half-moon edger or a sharp spade to cut a capital 'H' in the turf. Peel back the two flaps this creates then dig over the underlying soil before planting your bulbs. Remember to allow for the extra depth of the turves, which you simply fold back into place then firm down with your feet. To plant snowdrops in the green, remove a square of turf completely then tear it into pieces before firming them back, filling the cracks with loose soil. The grass will soon knit together again.

left: *Galanthus* 'Bellerina'; right: *G. nivalis*

garrya elliptica

Silk tassel bush · quinine bush A large evergreen shrub native to California and to other warm western parts of North America, the silk tassel bush or garrya was (re)discovered in 1827 by the plant hunter David Douglas on the south side of the Columbia River. (It was first found by Archibald Menzies on Captain George Vancouver's 1790–95 voyage in *The Discovery*.) Douglas named it after Nicholas Garry, deputy governor of the Hudson Bay Company, bestowing on him a greater honour than was at first realized. When the plant flowered for the first time in England in 1834 it was found to represent not just a new species, not just a whole new genus, but a brand new natural order (albeit a small one) promptly dubbed the Garryacae. This is the botanical equivalent of having a galaxy named after you instead of just a star.

Garrya elliptica has wavy-margined glossy dark green leaves that are matt grey green beneath. Plants are frost hardy but benefit from the shelter of a wall in cold areas. Shady walls are quite good enough for them, where they work well alongside the summer- and autumn-flowering clambering hydrangeas *H. anomala* subsp. *petiolaris* and *H. quercifolia* to bring interest to the more usual hollies, spotted laurels and variegated ivies. They tolerate salt air and are useful evergreens for seaside gardens where they can even be used as windbreaks, frost barely being a problem on the coast. (It's only the *combination* of biting wind on the leaves and extreme cold at the roots that sometimes puts paid to garryas inland).

From late autumn to the end of winter the bushes bear lengthening suede-green catkins of overlapping scales. These segments split apart from each other to reveal yellow-powdered ranks of silvery-green anthers. Bunches of these silky tassels drape the stems in profusion and easily reach a good 15–20/6–8in in length. A well hung specimen is a delight. For guaranteed satisfaction, the cultivar 'James Roof' packs an eye-popping 20–25cm/8–10in truss.

Pruning Tidy up plants by removing or shortening straggly growth after flowering.

Me Tarzan, you Jane Most flowers combine elements of both sexes. Some plants like the hazel carry separate male and female flowers and are described as monoecious. *Garrya elliptica* is dioecious, that is, plants carry the flowers of one sex exclusively. Sometimes only a man will do: for spectacular pollen-bearing tassels you must have a male specimen.

Heeled cuttings Cuttings are slow to root and are best taken in late summer and early autumn. Pull a side shoot gently away from a stem to carry off a small sliver of its bark. Trim this heel of older wood close to the base of the shoot, then shorten the whole thing to 12cm/5in or less by snipping off the tip just above a leaf node. To prevent moisture loss, pinch off any remaining leaves then pot it up in the usual way (see p.28). Because heel cuttings leave small jagged wounds in the parent plant's bark, a sensible approach is to prune out a wayward stem cleanly then use that as source material.

left: *Garrya elliptica* 'James Roof'

hamamelis

Soil and site Just as the cloying scent of daphne hints at poison within, so the sharpness of witch hazel indicates that acid soil is in order. All species of hamamelis prefer slightly acid to neutral soils which are moisture-retentive and rich in humus. A generous annual mulch of peat helps keep the ball rolling. Full sun to light shade give the most satisfactory results; too much shade inhibits flowering.

Beauty doesn't come cheap Propagation is out of the home gardener's realm since named varieties are spliced on to rootstocks of *Hamamelis virginiana*. Young grafted plants often fail, so it pays to invest in a large, well-grown specimen which is at least four or five years old. If you have inherited a plant on alkaline soil, treat it with sequestered iron to prevent the sickly premature yellowing of the leaves. If you have alkaline soil and you want to buy a witch hazel, forget it.

above: *Hamamelis* x *intermedia* 'Hiltingbury'

Witch hazel These hardy shrubs have a lovely spreading tree-like habit that makes them excellent free-standing specimens for the large or wilder-looking garden. Pruning spoils their graceful effect. Young twigs are covered in adolescent down and the matt mid-green 15cm/6in leaves, though coarse looking, are incredibly soft to the touch. End of season foliage ranges from clear bright yellow through honey gold to mixtures of flame orange, rich red and scarlet. Once coloured, the leaves put on a splendid show by hanging on tenaciously for a good four to six weeks before falling.

The flowers of the American native *Hamamelis virginiana* appear beside the leaves in autumn; those of the Chinese and Japanese witch hazels *H. mollis* and *H. japonica* appear on bare stems in winter. Many winter blooms are frost-resistant but these spidery clusters of thread-like petals are positively frost-proof. Their sharp invigorating tang in icy air is clean, refreshing and unmistakable: a cowslip sweetness swirls along on a zesty, antiseptic undercurrent.

Recollections triggered by smell are particularly evocative because they conjure up actual physical experience unsullied by language or spurious images. I first knew witch hazel not as the plant itself but as an astringent mint-green ointment kept in the cupboard under the stairs at my grandmother's house for applying liberally to cuts and grazes. I couldn't put the stinging sensation into words then, but the memory of it remains painfully clear even today. In spite of this, I find witch hazels themselves entrancing because their scent unlocks the floodgates to many fond childhood memories too.

The most desirable plants are hybrids of *H. mollis* and *H. japonica*. *H.* x *intermedia* 'Pallida' has sulphur yellow flowers 3cm/1¼in across in dense clusters and warm butter yellow autumn colour. *H.* x *i.* 'Vesna' has looser, shaggily held petals which are orange at the tip darkening to red at the base and look distinctly volcanic. *H.* x *i.* 'Diane' has coral red blooms and larger than average leaves, which turn yellow, orange and deep red in autumn before falling when a uniform nut brown.

Planting witch hazels next to dense glossy evergreens lends form and substance to the garden picture and helps visually to 'ground' the intense winter flower colour. It also provides good foliage contrast from spring to autumn. *Rhododendron bureaui* has dark polished leaves cloaked in rusty red fur beneath. It carries rose and crimson flowers from mid to late spring and makes an ideal companion on acid soils. On neutral soil go for the Mexican orange (*Choisya ternata*) which has citrus-scented white flowers from mid spring onwards. Viticella Group clematis can also be used creatively (see p.21).

helleborus

The secret's in the soil These shade lovers will tolerate acidity but they are happier in neutral to limy soil that is moist, fertile and rich in humus. Spent mushroom compost is the perfect soil conditioner when planting out as it contains gypsum, which is alkaline. Well-rotted manure is full of nutrients and never goes amiss. As hellebores have long fleshy roots, they bitterly resent disturbance, so although you can propagate them by division in late spring or in autumn, it is better to provide them with ideal conditions and encourage self seeding. If you grow several forms together you'll create your own unique varieties. Transplant chance seedlings with as large a rootball as possible so they don't realize what you're up to.

Fine tuning Mulch low-growing varieties with chipped bark to reduce mud-splashing during rain. To produce absolutely pristine specimens for vases, protect the blooms with a sheet of Perspex on wire supports and wait until all the buds on a stem have opened before cutting. The flowers last longer if the cut end of the stem is quickly seared in the flame of a cigarette lighter. Float a handful of stemless blooms in a shallow bowl of water for a breathtaking table centre.

left and right: *Helleborus orientalis* cultivars

Hellebores are so beautiful and long lasting they would be impossible to overlook even in mid summer. That they flower continuously throughout the winter is nothing short of miraculous.

Christmas rose · Lenten rose

Like snowflakes, each hellebore you see looks strikingly different to the last yet the family resemblance is unmistakable. This popular genus of hardy perennials has innumerable named varieties but only about a dozen species, of which *Helleborus niger* and *H. orientalis* give most pleasure to gardeners. The Christmas rose is predominantly white – *niger* refers to the black roots – while the Lenten or Easter rose and its hybrids can be white, yellow, pink, red, purple-black and, most remarkable still, apple-green. This *fin de siècle* flower colour is the clue to every hellebore's extraordinary resilience to snow and ice. Botanically speaking their petals are the much tougher sepals, protective scales forming the case of the flower bud, which have taken on the role of attracting pollinating insects. The true petals have become tiny nectar-producing organs instead and can just be seen encircling the showy central cluster of yellow stamens.

Probably the finest form of *H. niger* is 'Potter's Wheel', which from early winter to early spring produces 10–12cm/4–5in flowers carried well above the evergreen foliage on sturdy and erect stems up to 30cm/12in in height. Smaller and daintier 4–7cm/1½–3in flowers are the norm and double (multi-petalled) and dwarf forms exist.

H. orientalis flowers a little later from mid winter to mid spring, so grow both species for a gloriously long season. Orientalis hybrids are legion, so be guided by your own judgment; beauty is in the eye of the beholder and an attractive garden-centre seedling can have just as much charm as anything named after 'Lady Muck'. Deep purples like 'Nocturne' and 'Saturn' are exquisite close up, but don't expect to admire them from afar; you'll gaze out of the window for them in vain, like looking for a black cat in a dark room. Lighter, brighter colours are wiser garden choices. Glossy yellows light up bare soil and shine through frost. Warm pinks are an unexpected joy in the midst of winter and some strains resemble giant apple blossoms with all but the margin of each petal beautifully freckled red. The vivid, some might say day-glo, greens show up surprisingly well and always arouse some comment.

For bolder, more architectural effects spare a thought for one more species, the stinking hellebore *H. foetidus*. A sterling year-round foliage plant with distinctive cannabis-shaped leaves that are dark, leathery and evergreen, in mid winter it bears masses of cup-shaped Chartreuse flowers cascading from stems as tall as 80cm/32in. 'Wester Flisk' is an outstanding cultivar with elegant red-rimmed flowers. Wow!

iris unguicularis

Propagation The gung-ho approach is to hack up an old clump with a sharp spade after flowering. A more satisfactory method is to dig the whole clump out with a fork and gently tease the rhizomes apart before replanting. This requires a little more patience but the new plants are less congested and will cover a much wider area. They are also healthier and faster to flower because the rhizomes aren't so traumatized.

Cut flowers There are two things you will notice when you bring the blooms indoors. The first is their delicate orange-blossom and honey fragrance. The second is the fact that the 'stem' isn't made of stem at all but of the same material as the petals. It is actually the elongated tube of the flower and only meets the real scape or stem at ground level. No wonder these irises look so delicate.

Algerian iris To be really free-flowering from winter to spring the rhizomes of this North African and Eastern Mediterranean gem require a good summer baking. Pop them hard up against your hottest and sunniest wall, preferably in poor soil, neglect shamelessly and don't add water. This sounds like a recipe for disaster. Not so. It's a perfect illustration of how the key to successful gardening lies in finding either the right place for any given plant or the right plant for a particular place. If you fatten it up on an over-rich diet the Algerian iris puts all its energy into the slender, arching, evergreen leaves which can reach a length of 60cm/24in and form an untidy mound to a height of 30cm/12in or so. Not only does this more or less obscure the few flowers the plant bothers to produce, but the juicy roots and lush top growth become prone to rot and frost damage. You must be cruel to be kind. In spartan conditions resembling its native habitat, *Iris unguicularis* has short tidy foliage and it is reliably hardy, long lived and floriferous.

The violet-purple, lilac-blue or white flowers are 5–7cm/2–3in across and rarely exceed 15cm/6in in height. They have three broadening backward curving petals or 'falls', and three which are more tapering and erect – the 'standards'. It's the classic iris structure, but fine boned, wide eyed and demure. All the petals are exquisitely veined and there is a splash of white and gold where the falls flex in the middle. All told, they're as chic as Audrey Hepburn in Givenchy.

I. u. 'Walter Butt' is especially vigorous, and has palest silver-lilac flowers with large falls and small standards, which appear in quantity from late autumn onwards. Winter-blooming 'Alba' is creamy white with a greeny-yellow line running down the centre of the falls. *I. u.* 'Unguicularis Marginata' has lilac-blue petals edged in white. 'Variegata' has mottled flowers with purple streaks on a lavender background. 'Mary Barnard' is darkest violet-purple so the blaze on the falls makes an especially dashing contrast. The final three generally bloom from late winter into spring.

jasminum nudiflorum

Winter jasmine This widely planted wall shrub is one of the all-time greats. Bursting with vim and vigour, and indestructibly hardy, it is a sight for sore eyes on dreary winter days. It can bring the darkest of corners and the coldest of walls to life, and well-grown specimens will pour out cascades of flowers from late autumn right through until spring.

Flaunting the bold imperial yellow of its Chinese homeland, it has a long history in the Orient both as a garden plant and as a cut flower, and it is mentioned in literature dating back to the sixteenth century. In floral art it was traditionally combined with apricot blossom, daphne and camellias. The West was slow to catch on but it was finally noted by Dr Alexander von Bunge in Beijing in 1830–31. It was introduced to England in 1844 by Robert Fortune who found it growing in nurseries and gardens around Shanghai. Plant-hunting wasn't always tough work.

The buds are red-splashed at the tips but the five- or six-petalled flowers open pure yellow and resemble tiny primroses. These exquisite miniatures are borne in profusion but, alas, they have no smell. For exotic perfume you need the white-flowered summer to autumn blooming *Jasminum officinale* instead. The whippy stems are bare in winter but they are an attractive bottle-green and make a perfect backdrop to the flowers. The 2.5cm/1in leaves appear in spring and are carried in groups of three. Those of *J. nudiflorum* 'Aureum' are generously splashed yellow and make the shrub look sun-dappled. Each leaf of *J. n.* 'Mystique' has a narrow silver-white margin sometimes tinged pink.

Smooth-stemmed Oriental beauty seeks horny-handed son of toil for mutually beneficial flower arrangement. Must be into strict pruning.

General care Variegated forms can scorch in summer so use them to brighten up the darker parts of your garden. Propagate by taking 10cm/4in semi-ripe cuttings in summer or by layering in autumn. Plants can be used as large-scale groundcover down sloping banks where they will root as they go.

Pruning and training To grow a young winter jasmine against a wall or a fence, tie in the main stems for support but let the floppy sideshoots arch outwards. When flowering is over cut all stems back by two thirds and tie in the remaining new growth fanwise to create a strong framework.

Established plants should have the number of woody main stems reduced by a third annually. Select the oldest ones and prune them to within 10cm/4in of the ground. Tie back the previous year's top growth on the remaining stems as before then tie in new basal growth at the same time. This way plants stay within bounds and always look attractive. Tiddling about like a hairdresser results in the ugly bird's-nest effect that gives jasmine a bad name.

lonicera fragrantissima

Winter honeysuckle Honeysuckle? Winter? Some genera are more versatile than you imagine. The Japanese honeysuckle *Lonicera japonica* 'Aureoreticulata' has emerald evergreen leaves which are meshed with golden yellow veins. It flowers in summer so I'm not going to talk about it here, even though it looks beautiful climbing on tree trunks in winter. People are often surprised to learn that some honeysuckles keep their foliage all year round. The stunning evergreen *L. nitida* 'Ernest Wilson' has tiny box-like leaves and is excellent for topiary. *L. n.* 'Baggesen's Gold' is rich butter yellow, and both forms make hardy and durable hedges (and ones which deer will never eat). I won't mention those either, even though honeysuckle is so little known as a shrub. No. All I want to look at is a semi-evergreen shrubby honeysuckle that flowers in the middle of winter. But you already guessed.

Western horticulture has a lot to thank the Chinese for. *L. fragrantissima* is another of the plants Robert Fortune picked up on one of his garden sorties. Along with *L. standishii* it was packed off to England in 1845. Superficially they are very similar, but there are subtle differences to consider before making your final choice. *L. fragrantissima* has a delicate spreading habit and retains more of its oval blue-green leaves through winter. *L. standishii* has the same dusty-looking grey stems, which are twiggy and somewhat brittle, but it has a more upright growth pattern that makes it less prone to breakages. Also, it starts into flower a fraction earlier in late autumn, but both species bloom more or less continuously throughout winter and into early spring. A hybrid between the two called *L.* x *purpusii* 'Winter Beauty' is intermediate in shape with a rounded silhouette, and it is a little more vigorous than its parents. Its new shoots and young foliage have an attractive purple cast.

All three species bear incredibly fragrant tubular white flowers. Because honeysuckle is so quintessentially the smell of summertime, wafts of it in the depths of winter come as a huge psychological boost. It lifts your mind out of dark and despondency and carries your thoughts to balmier days of warmth and sunshine.

The Breath of Flowers is farre Sweeter in the Aire (where it comes and Goes, like the Warbling of Musick) than in the hand.

Sir Francis Bacon (1561–1626)

Site These small shrubs are very hardy, tolerate dry soils well, and grow in sun or shade. Semi-ripe cuttings taken in late summer root easily.

Pruning To encourage ongoing renewal from the base of older plants, remove up to a quarter of the old stems by taking them back to within a bud or two of the ground. Shorten up to a third of the remaining branches by cutting them back to just above a vigorous new outward-facing shoot. This gives you a strong, healthy shrub, which nevertheless has a relaxed and open-looking habit. Left alone, main stems are altogether less sturdy and top growth is inclined to be congested – not a good combination.

The bigger picture Winter-flowering honeysuckles are dull for much of the year, and their brittle stems make them poor hosts for climbers, but they do have a useful duty to perform. The spreading branches of well-pruned specimens provide discreet, perfectly camouflaged support for top-heavy flowers on tall thin stalks. Herbaceous perennials like larkspur, lilies, phlox and the peach-leaved bellflower *Campanula persicifolia*, meld beautifully together grown round these shrubs. The honeysuckle disappears; the summer border looks stunning; you don't have to do any staking. Perfect.

left: *Lonicera* x *purpusii* 'Winter Beauty'

mahonia

Soil and site Because mahonias are tough enough to be used regularly for amenity planting by local authorities many people hold them in low esteem. But take the trouble to plant them in rich moist soil with a little shade and they'll earn your respect and admiration in next to no time.

Pruning To produce fresh young foliage on *Mahonia aquifolium* shear it almost to ground level every two or three years once flowering is over. Tall-growing plants like *M. x media* 'Charity' are best left untouched; gauntness is part of their charm. If you need to keep a mature specimen within bounds then completely remove an elderly stem or two once in a very long while. Don't disfigure the poor thing by hacking it about each year.

Propagation Suckers from *M. aquifolium* are easily pulled up and replanted. Cuttings can be taken from taller species in late summer. For quick results though, wiggle a young stem out of the ground like a loose tooth and replant it immediately where it is to grow, shorn of all leaves. Do this in autumn.

right: *Mahonia japonica*

Mahonia These plants make a fine architectural statement all year round. Their leaves are pinnate, that is, they consist of a series of leaflets on each side of a common stalk. A little softer and less uptight than holly leaves, individual leaflets are tough, shiny and spiky but, because they are carried in fronds, mahonias have a light and airy habit with none of that dark solidity so common to evergreens. They bring backbone to borders and strike a grace note in shrubberies.

In winter they excel themselves. The leaves of some species colour richly in autumn and prolonged frost can even turn them bright red before they revert back to green in spring. They all carry small sweetly scented yellow flowers in long tapering spikes, racemes, or loose frothy panicles. Edible blue-black berries, often with a powdery white bloom, follow on.

Mahonia x media 'Charity' has an upright, stately habit and is arguably the finest variety. The leaves are 50cm/20in or so long and sprout in well-spaced whorls around the stems and in rosettes at the tips. The racemes are carried at first in erect bunches and the deep yellow flowers open from the bottom up, growing longer, slacker and more pendulous with age. *M. x m.* 'Buckland' is somewhat smaller but a more significant proportion of the leaves turn orange and yellow in the cold. *M. japonica* flowers from mid winter into spring and has luscious lemon-yellow racemes with a strong lily-of-the-valley fragrance. This is the smell that puzzles city-dwellers as they march past municipal shrubberies on their way to work. The leaves often turn a magnificent winter red, as do those of *M. aquifolium*, the Oregon grape, which only starts flowering very late in winter. Its sharp-tasting fruit are definitely worth cooking with. You're unlikely to have enough for jam so slip what you can gather in an apple pie. This low-growing American native is a valuable suckering ground-cover shrub for the larger garden. 'Smaragd' has bright emerald green leaves and especially large panicles of bright yellow flowers, the foliage of *M. a.* 'Atropurpurea' turns purple in winter.

I can resist everything except temptation.

Oscar Wilde (1854–1900)

petasites fragrans

Perfect planting Waterside giants like *Gunnera manicata* and *Lysichiton* (p.70) can look seriously out of scale with their surroundings unless keyed into the landscape by a mass of smaller yet equally bold foliage. Winter heliotrope does the trick. In small gardens it is an exciting and unusual container specimen for a shady spot where nothing else will grow.

Propagation As male and female flower-heads are carried on separate plants, garden species rarely set seed – but a little piece of rhizome can go an awfully long way.

Soil and site Plant winter heliotrope in rich moist soil in dappled or full shade. Then stand well back.

Winter heliotrope Beware! Gardeners are drawn to this plant like moths to a flame. But is it a wildflower, a garden plant, a conservatory specimen or a weed? If you worry about mint running riot and marigolds seeding too freely then winter heliotrope will give you nightmares. Admire its many talents in other people's gardens but leave it well alone. If you take a more robust attitude to life and if you have the wilder sort of garden, then you might just want to give it a go...

Petasites fragrans is a native wildflower in Italy, Sicily and Mediterranean North Africa. It was brought into cultivation in 1806 and became a popular Victorian pot plant on account of its vanilla and cherry pie fragrance. It was treated as an exotic at first, but it's hardier than its origins suggest – it is also a rampant spreader. It soon ran riot in gardens and escaped back into the wild with a vengeance. It is now commonly naturalized along roadsides in warm sheltered woodlands throughout western Europe and is always looking to hitch a lift.

The young flower-heads are distinctly eerie. In the middle of winter, knobbly clusters of anaemic buds shoot up from below ground on short fleshy stalks. More than anything else they resemble morel mushrooms, and this fungal appearance is reinforced by the initial absence of any foliage. Before the kidney shaped leaves emerge and expand a few weeks later, the flower stalks lengthen considerably and their pink and white blooms fill the air with an unexpected sweetness.

Soft light green on top, white and furry beneath, the leaves ultimately reach 20–25cm/8–10in in diameter and stand umbrella-like on upright stems a foot or so high. Because they emerge so early and shade the ground so effectively nothing else on their patch stands a chance. In large gardens, colonies make an excellent weed smotherer and dramatic ground cover for areas that are hard to reach and would otherwise look unkempt. In small gardens the plant's rampaging tendency can make it a troublesome weed in its own right. Are you and your garden big enough to take it on?

prunus x subhirtella 'autumnalis'

Higan cherry Too many of the ornamental cherries now in cultivation are knicker-pink 'quickies', double-flowered varieties that bloom suddenly and profusely in mid to late spring then hurl down their petals to litter the streets. They are spectacular in their moment of glory but they are singularly lacking in charm and they are poor company for the rest of the year. Wham, bam, no thank you, ma'am.

The Higan is a different kettle of fish. It is also known as the autumn cherry and as the winter cherry. These names give you a fair idea of its long flowering season but don't do it full justice as it actually goes on into spring too. Not all the flowers bloom at once, though – that would be asking too much. The pink buds open intermittently from late autumn to early spring in little showers of fragile white blossom.

It has a spreading or gently weeping habit and, like most cherries, will ultimately attain a height of 6–7.5m/20–25ft or so.

This takes 25 years at least, so don't panic. It is usually grafted on to an understock of the gean or wild cherry, *Prunus avium*, and sold ready trained as a tree, but nurseries also offer it as a multi-stemmed shrub. The dark green leaves have toothed margins and are pale bronze in spring turning red, orange and yellow before falling in autumn.

The almond-scented flowers are small, semi-double and cup-shaped with somewhat frilled petals. *P.* x *subhirtella* 'Autumnalis Rosea' has petals delicately flushed rose-pink. They grow in twos and threes from buds in the leaf axils and the first blossom appears alongside the autumn foliage. Fresh flowers appear in succession during winter mild spells and the delicacy of the sprays is breathtaking. If severe weather strikes in mid winter the tree simply puts its schedule temporarily on hold, becoming dormant, and holding its blossom in reserve for when conditions warm up again at the end of the season.

Location, location For plenty of flowers and for good autumn leaf colour the Higan cherry needs a position in full sun. Like any tree it should be planted at least one and half its ultimate height away from your home.

Pruning Leave well alone except to remove dead or damaged shoots.

Forcing However cold it is outside, bare sprays cut for vases will soon burst into blossom indoors.

Special effects Cherries are often grown as lawn specimens. A large and loose drift of small-flowered bulbs naturalized beneath creates a real dynamic between the earth and the sky. Large means the size and shape of a shadow cast by the tree, not the size of a posy for a grave. Colchicums (p.128) look good in autumn; snowdrops (p.30) are the obvious winter choice; crocuses (p.61) are perfect in spring. It is preferable to stick to one variety of each species but by all means plant a seasonal succession of drifts.

right: *Prunus* x *subhirtella* 'Autumnalis Rosea'

pulmonaria

Soil and site To produce big fine leaves and good tall flowers *Pulmonaria saccharata* needs humus-rich soil that is moist and fertile. It gives its best in dappled shade where the silvery foliage really shines out. If you can't offer optimum conditions then opt for *P. officinalis* instead. This tolerates full sun just so long as the soil never bakes dry, and handles dryish conditions just so long as it has shade. Better a thriving small plant than an ailing large one.

Powdery mildew Powdery mildew affects the leaves of moisture-lovers when they get too *dry* at the roots, especially if the air surrounding the foliage is humid. It is commonly seen in forget-me-nots and asters. Remove affected leaves and keep the plants well watered. Don't use the rose of a watering can to sprinkle the foliage from above. Keep humidity to a minimum by gently pouring water straight on to the soil from the spout. The long-term solution is to lift the plants and move them somewhere more salubrious.

Propagation is easy If you lift and divide even the smallest clump of Pulmonarias after flowering you will have more small plants than you know what to do with.

Perfect planting If you grow pulmonarias over narcissus bulbs your soldiers and sailors give way to daffodil trumpets, then the daffodil leaves fade inconspicuously amidst the lungwort's fresh summer foliage, which carries you right through to next winter.

left and right: *Pulmonaria saccharata*

Lungwort · Soldiers & sailors · Jerusalem sage

Many plants which were once the stock-in-trade of herbalists have the specific epithet *officinalis*, 'of the shop'. Inspired by Paracelsus, the Doctrine of Signatures followed by sixteenth- and seventeenth-century herbalists held that plants that resembled specific parts of the human body could be used medicinally to cure their disorders or ailments. So the walnut with its hard skull-like shell protecting a soft brain-like kernel was clearly good for your noggin, while lungwort's blotched and spotty leaves were proof positive of its efficacy in treating diseases of the pulmonary tract. Oh, that life were so simple.

Pulmonaria officinalis is the most widely cultivated species and its nickname comes from the funnel-shaped flowers that change from soldier pink to sailor blue as they mature. They are vigorous in any good moist soil, succeeding best of all in shade. They are remarkably hardy. Their loose rosettes of hairy, silver-spotted foliage make versatile and extremely handsome semi-evergreen groundcover, which fits as comfortably into the smartest borders as into wild gardens and woodland settings. If you already grow pulmonaria, chances are it is this one. Chances are too that you've occasionally seen plants which are larger, lusher and far more silvery-leaved than yours. Ah well, perhaps their owners have greener fingers. Ah well, rubbish! They're growing a different plant.

Where *P. officinalis* is a good plant, *P. saccharata*, Jerusalem sage, is a great one. Its leaves, at 20–25cm/8–10in long, are twice the size. It is much more heavily frosted with silver – or indeed with sugar. Its flowers are carried on taller stalks, easily 30cm/12in, sometimes as high as 45cm/18in. Regardless of the weather it starts blooming in the second half of winter and carries on till late spring. Like all pulmonarias, once flowering is over it diverts its energy into producing a fresh flush of brilliantly marked leaves to replace last year's old-timers.

Argentea Group plants have been specially selected for their large splotches of overlapping spots which make the leaves almost entirely silver. *P. officinalis* 'Sissinghurst White' has large white flowers the size of pearls enhancing silver-freckled foliage; *P. s.* 'Alba' has smaller white flowers but more metallic-looking leaves. The characteristic mauve-pink to purple-blue flowers are borne in profusion on *P.* 'Margery Fish' which is full of vigour and deservedly one of the most popular cultivars. Whichever form you choose, prepare for gasps of admiration.

Free pH testing Take a leisurely stroll round your neighbourhood one Sunday afternoon and peer into everyone's front garden. If you see healthy, well-established specimens of rhododendron, azalea, heather and pieris then you're on acid enough soil. If not, not.

General cultivation Light shade is preferred, but full sun will be tolerated if there is adequate moisture. Deep mulching with peat or compost in autumn enriches the soil and protects shallow roots from winter frost and summer sun. Remove the flowers as they fade. This keeps plants more vigorous by preventing seedheads from forming. If your garden soil is unsuitable, grow them in large pots of ericaceous compost.

Pruning Rhododendrons in open ground need little attention. Keep container-grown specimens to size by cutting them back a little after flowering every few years.

rhododendron nobleanum group

Rhododendron You either love them or loathe them. Prejudice can easily blind us to a plant's true merits, so let's take an impartial look. Rhododendrons are ghastly dull evergreens. Once a year their huge vulgar flowers unbalance the scale of your garden and clash horribly in colour with everything around them. It defeats me why people muck around with their soil to grow them in the first place. Then again... What other shrub, apart from the rose, comes in such an amazing range of shapes and colours? The best way to appreciate rhododendrons is to plant them en masse. They look after themselves and different species flower throughout the year. The leaves are handsome and smart. Mmm...

Now for some facts. Rhododendrons can be vivid orange, scarlet or purple but they can also be subtle mixes of virgin white, palest peach and softest pink. Some have flower trusses like footballs, others have loose bunches of elegant bells. They needn't jar with anything. Acid soil is essential. Whatever stupid advice you follow to grow them in alkaline soil will end in tears.

In districts where rhododendrons do well they are often overused. If the flowering season isn't staggered, large plantings look dark and monotonous for too much of the year. In a massive woodland garden a dedicated area can be a knockout to visit in late spring or early summer but small gardens really need a lot of other plants mixed in for greater foliage contrast and year-round flower effect.

Sceptics and fans alike can benefit from planting Nobleanum Group rhododendrons. They are slow-growing, so they live happily in containers. Their long narrow leaves are white and furry underneath. They bloom in winter when all flower colour is welcome. *R.* 'Nobleanum Album' has pink-flushed buds which open pure lily white. The flowers of *R.* 'Nobleanum Venustum' have shell pink rims fading almost to white at the rose-speckled throat. *R.* 'Nobleanum Coccineum' has scarlet buds and rich rose-coloured petals with pale pink throats splashed crimson. Everybody happy?

sarcococca

Winter box · Sweet box This low-growing evergreen shrub is related to box, that mainstay of the English formal garden. It is a less suitable subject for intricate topiary because it is looser, longer-leaved and faster-growing than its cousin, but it is an excellent alternative for edging pathways and beds when quick results are needed. Winter box will never give you the hard outlines and dense leaf cover for which the real McCoy is so rightly prized, but on the other hand its foliage has none of that acrid foxy tang that many people find beyond the pale. Where box is a dapper little dandy doused in *eau de Reynard*, sarcococca is a quietly dignified charmer with a little something up his sleeve. Throughout the second half of winter the air is filled with a deliciously clean, penetrating honeysuckle fragrance. And people are damned if they can find where it's coming from.

The flowers on sarcococca are tiny white tassels consisting of styles and stamens only. No petals. No sepals. Nothing to write home about. The leaves protect them from the elements and more or less shield them from view. The scent is so amazing that the mind's eye is convinced it must belong to some large and glamorous bloom. It takes a great deal of patient searching and a huge leap of imagination to track it down to its source. If for no other reason than to baffle the uninitiated, this is one plant you simply must grow.

Reaching a maximum height of 1.2–1.5m/4–5ft *Sarcococca confusa* is the tallest and bulkiest species with narrow leaves up to 5cm/2in long. *S. ruscifolia* is the next size down; its leaves are more sharply pointed and it is the only one to have red berries. *S. hookeriana* var. *digyna* has pinkish flowers and possibly the sweetest scent; it has the characteristic purple-black 1cm/½in berries which take the best part of a year to ripen. The humble *S. h.* var. *humilis* bravely grows above 60cm/2ft; the creamy-white flowers bloom alongside last year's round, glistening fruit.

Soil and site Sarcococca prefers light shade, where it can tolerate root competition and remarkably dry soil.

Propagation Sarcococca becomes bushier by sending up new shoots from its slowly creeping root system. These are easy to remove with a sharp knife and transplant in early spring or late summer.

Pruning For an informal shrub simply remove weak shoots and tired old wood once flowering is over. For a neater, denser specimen or to train a hedge, you should also reduce the previous year's growth by half each spring to encourage stems to branch and to promote new growth from the base.

Another surprise For a larger evergreen hedge, also with the unexpected bonus of scent, plant *Elaeagnus pungens* which has dark green leaves tinged white beneath and tiny fragrant flowers in autumn. There are a number of yellow and cream variegated cultivars. The hybrid *E.* x *ebbingei* has foliage that is silvery when young.

right: *Sarcococca hookeriana*

stachyurus

Planting notes A woodland native, stachyurus enjoys a deep, leafy, preferably acid soil that is moist but well drained. So long as its roots are happy it does as well in full sun as in light dappled shade. In a shrubbery dark evergreens are the best foil for the flowers and it is an especially good winter leaven in a lump of summer-flowering rhododendrons. For the added dimension of scent, underplant it with *Sarcococca hookeriana* var. *humilis* (p.45). It is also a good solo specimen shrub for herbaceous borders in winter. In the summer it can act either as a discreet support for tall perennials or alternatively as a host for climbers that can be cut back in autumn.

Pruning Cut out weak stems on young plants after flowering. Keep established specimens in check by shortening over-long branches. Mature shrubs can be renovated by removing a few old stems.

Propagation Semi-ripe cuttings can be taken in summer but are slow to root.

Stachyurus The pendulous flower clusters of this extremely hardy oriental shrub provide a long-lasting display from late autumn well into spring. Formed in the leaf axils of all branches that are two or more years old, they are revealed when their cloak of yellowing foliage is whipped away by the wind. They hang like strings of beads all winter through, their stalks slowly lengthening until the waxy primrose-yellow cup-shaped blooms finally burst out of their jade-green buds in late winter and early spring. With the light behind them the translucent flowers glow out of the gloom like Japanese paper lanterns. These delicate, graceful catkins have an uncanny air of peace and tranquillity. Never mind the swirling icy gales howling round the rest of the garden, a Zen-like aura of stillness and serenity seems to enfold and protect the bushes at all times. What could their secret be? Stachyurus comes from the Greek *stachys*, a spike, and *oura*, a tail. If you shake a branch you'll find that each dangling shoot is in fact as stiff as a board and quite immovable. (The noise you just heard was a hallelujah from flower arrangers everywhere.)

A fully grown specimen of *Stachyurus chinensis* stands about 2m/6ft 6in tall and has an open, sprawling habit. Young branches have a purple-brown tinge that looks well with the flowers. The grey-green leaves are veined maroon and are up to 15cm/6in long; they appear after the flowers in spring. The drooping racemes are about 12.5cm/5in long and hold around 30–36 individual flowers. S. 'Magpie' is a less vigorous variegated form with each leaf splashed pale green at the centre and generously margined ivory and cream; its leaves acquire pink tints with age. Somewhat rare, it is highly sought-after, as it brightens the garden both in winter and in summer.

S. *praecox* hails from Japan; it is a little shorter than its cousins but forms a more erect shrub. It has reddish-brown twigs and carries no more than 24 paler yellow flowers in racemes around 7cm/3in long. The buds open a week or two earlier than those of the Chinese species.

above: *Sachyurus praecox*

viburnum x bodnantense

Viburnum The evergreen laurustinus, *Viburnum tinus*, has pink buds opening into white flowers from winter to spring and shiny blue-black fruit in autumn. In late spring and early summer the common guelder rose, *V. opulus*, bears a profusion of white lacecap flowerheads which turn to glistening bunches of bright red berries in the autumn; the maple-like foliage turns yellow and scarlet before falling. The barren *V. o.* 'Roseum', the snowball bush, compensates for its lack of fruit by producing spectacular pom-pom flowerheads like mop-head hydrangeas. Though the flowers of *V. davidii*, with its dark green pleated leaves, are nothing like so showy, female plants startle onlookers in autumn with clusters of metallic turquoise to purple fruit on orange-red stalks. *Viburnum* x *bodnantense* however, a hybrid raised by the second Lord Aberconway at Bodnant in North Wales, is in a league of its own. Exhibited for the first time in 1947, it is perhaps the most vigorous frost-resistant, sweetly scented winter-flowering shrub ever.

Viburnum x *bodnantense*, though gaunt and spindly as a baby shrublet, eventually forms a dense clump of strong, slightly arching stems which can be up to 3m/10ft high. Its toothed lance-shaped leaves are light green tinged with bronze when they emerge, but quickly turn dark green. They are about 10cm/4in long when mature. The tubular flowers are carried in thick clusters on the bare stems from late autumn to early spring. Should one crop be ruined by frost, another will follow swiftly on its heels in the next mild spell. The sweet, nutty scent is reminiscent of honey and marzipan. Though less penetrating than that of *Daphne odorata* it is altogether warmer and more delicious. *V.* x *b.* 'Deben' has pink buds opening into pure white blooms; *V.* x *b.* 'Charles Lamont' has candy pink flowers; *V.* x *b.* 'Dawn', the most commonly grown cultivar, has gloriously rich rose-pink clusters becoming softer and paler with age.

below: *Viburnum* x *bodnantense* 'Dawn'

If you plant only one winter-flowering shrub, this has got to be the one.

Don't worry, be happy Viburnums thrive in any soil, in any site. They are fully hardy and trouble-free. Let them look after you.

Pruning A young plant is best left to its own devices. As an adolescent bush approaches your preferred height keep it to size not by shortening the branches but by completely removing about a quarter of the old stems each year. This retains the elegant habit, lets in light and air, and rejuvenates the plant on a rolling four to five year basis.

Propagation Take heeled cuttings of semi-ripe wood in late summer or early autumn.

Perfect planting This is an excellent shrub for the back of a border. It shines over bare dark earth in winter then forms a handsome green backdrop for the flowers of late spring and summer. For the fullest appreciation of its fragrance make it part of a boundary planting.

spring

Spring drew on. The garden on a sunny day began even to be pleasant and genial, and a greenness grew over those brown beds, which, freshening daily, suggested the thought that Hope traversed them at night, and left each morning brighter traces of her steps.

Charlotte Brontë (1816–1855) *Jane Eyre*

left: *Pulsatilla vulgaris*; above: *Crocus tommasinianus*

Cultivation Bugle prefers a moist soil and partial shade – just the sort of conditions found between herbaceous perennials in a well-tended border.

Propagation The leaf rosettes of bugle spread by sending out long shoots called stolons. These grow new plants at the tips which then root into the soil. Young plants are easily lifted and replanted. To propagate, just tear up a handful and plant it elsewhere.

Problems Bugle is susceptible to powdery mildew on dry soils. And under optimum conditions it can become a bit of a problem itself. Don't worry, world domination is easily thwarted with a handfork.

A good mixer Leggy architectural plants such as cordyline, phormium and mahonia (p.39) particularly benefit from low underplanting as it keeps their lines clean. A layer of bugle over autumn- and winter-flowering bulbs works well alongside larger evergreen ground-cover such as bergenia (p.20) and pulmonaria (p.43). Why not stick some narcissus (p.72) under the pulmonaria then work in a few choice summer blooms?

ajuga reptans

Bugle Ta-da-da-ra-da-ta-ta! Roll up, roll up ladies and gentlemen. See the greatest ground-cover plant in the world. The leaves are brighter than a harlequin's coat! The flowers are piercing blue! It's so versatile and pretty you just can't get enough of it. I give you... *Ajuga reptans!*

If you don't plant up all the ground in a bed or border then nature will step in and do it for you. Weed seeds and creeping grasses are always ready to fill a gap. If you don't evict them immediately they've got a foot in the door and soon begin to claim squatter's rights. You can hoe bare soil regularly to kill unwanted seedlings as they emerge. You can mulch it with bark chippings or coconut husks to prevent them getting a toe hold in the earth. You can painstakingly pull out grown weeds by hand. Or you can save yourself a lot of trouble by getting in ahead of them with a choice plant or two of your own.

Ram too many large plants close together though, and your garden loses all sense of grace, shape and rhythm. This is where 'ground-cover' plants come in – low-growing plants that punctuate the spaces between taller ones. Don't think of them as dull though. Respect them as much as every other plant you buy and apply your usual high artistic standards. They are the bottom tier of an elaborate cake, not the cardboard tray beneath.

A large clump of bugle is a spectacular sight in late spring. Whorls of bright blue tubular flowers are tightly packed on 10–15cm/4–6in high spikes that shimmer in profusion above the ground-hugging evergreen foliage. Not that evergreen has to mean green. *Ajuga reptans* 'Atropurpurea' has dark bronze-purple leaves, 'Bronze Beauty' is the same colour but with a distinctly metallic sheen. Variegated 'Burgundy Glow' is a beautiful green, white, pink and crimson. There are other flower colours too, 'Alba' is white, 'Rosea' mauve-pink.

akebia quinata

Chocolate vine · five-leaf akebia This vigorous semi-evergreen climber retains its foliage through all but the hardest of winters and is far tougher than it looks. If it loses its leaves, recovery is rapid; if prolonged frost cuts all the sinuous stems to the ground, it simply regrows from the base in a season. A mature plant can reach a height and spread of 6x6m/20x20ft but can easily be kept well within that.

The leaves are palmate, shaped like an open hand, with the five 4–7cm/1½–3in light green oval leaflets joined to the 7–12cm/3–5in leaf-stalks by little stems of their own. They are dainty and decorative individually, impressive en masse. At the risk of sounding stupid, *Akebia quinata* has the huge benefit of being evergreen without looking evergreen. Happy in sun or light shade, it is the perfect dense but casual-looking disguise for ugly walls and fences yet it looks remarkably pretty twining around rustic pergolas and peeping through ornamental trellis-work.

The chocolate vine is not self-clinging, but widely-spaced horizontal wires are all that are needed to help it clamber up an eyesore. It compares very favourably with ivy, whose clinging aerial roots can damage masonry and whose grim solidity invariably draws attention to whatever it is supposed to be hiding. Dark ivy's uptight habit defines boundaries; akebia's airy nonchalance diffuses light and makes outlines hazy.

Male and female flowers appear in mid to late spring on loose pendent racemes around 10cm/4in long. Remarkably exotic-looking for early blooms, they are such tough cookies because, like hellebores, their 'petals' are sepals. The cup-shaped females are chocolate-purple with violet pistils and measure about 3cm/1¼in across. They have a delicious spicy chocolate and vanilla aroma. With their chubby little reflexed petals, the smaller and paler males look more like berries than flowers. The fruits themselves are large and sausage-shaped, 7–10cm/3–4in long, they ripen to a murky purple in summertime. Not only are they unusual and decorative, but they have a culinary use as well. Almost cloyingly sweet by themselves they are a delicious ingredient in fruit salad.

Pruning Keep plants trim by shearing them closer to their support every few years once flowering is over.

Fruity stuff The chocolate vine is self-sterile: a plant's male flowers can't pollinate its own females. Fruiting requires fertilisation, so grow two plants, that aren't related, side by side. Cuttings from the same parent plant will be clones, so obviously won't do. Buy your plants from a nursery selling two different, clearly identified strains.

More chocolate? If *Akebia quinata* has whetted your appetite, try growing *Cosmos atrosanguineus*. This 75cm/30in tall perennial has chocolate-scented flowers from mid summer to autumn. They are shallowly cup-shaped, chocolatey maroon in colour and 4–5cm/1½–2in in diameter. Cocoa husks are now sold for use as a mulch and soil conditioner. A thick layer on your borders makes your garden smell truly scrumptious all year round.

aquilegia vulgaris

Columbine · granny's bonnet These exquisitely shaped and beautifully coloured flowers have been growing in gardens for centuries; written accounts date the aquilegia to 1310 at least, and it is mentioned by both Geoffrey Chaucer and William Shakespeare. By the end of the sixteenth century there were already a great many cultivated varieties. 'These flowers', recorded John Gerard, 'are of colour sometimes blewe, at other times of a red or purple, often white or of mixt colours, which to distinguish severally would be to small purpose, being things so familiarly known to all.' If anything, they're a somewhat unfamiliar sight today, which is rather a shame, and a bit of a mystery too, as they're terribly easy to grow.

Some species are native to North America, some to Europe. Essentially *Aquilegia vulgaris* is the wild European columbine and has glaucous blue-green foliage. Lobed, triangular leaflets are carried in threes and the overall effect is of a large maidenhair fern. The flowers appear in late spring and early summer. Colour is naturally variable and there are purple, violet, blue, pink and white forms. The Latin name, from *aquila*, an eagle, and the common name, from *columba*, a dove, are references to the shape. Depending on your point of view, their flared petals with hollow, pointed nectaries sticking out behind like spurs resemble either a gathering of doves (outstretched wings, inflated chest) or the heads of eagles (mane of feathers, large hooked beak). While the distinctive nodding blooms of the species have an elegant simplicity, the elaborately wrought flowerheads of modern cultivars are simply astonishing. *A. v.* 'Magpie' looks dapper with dark purple outer petals and spurs, the white forward-pointing inner petals have darker purple throats that are almost black. Girly *A. v.* 'Nora Barlow' has heavily double rose-pink flower pom-poms comprised of spiky petals tipped white and palest green. In *A. v.* 'William Guiness Doubles' the broad pleated and quilled petals form complex blooms somewhat resembling dahlias, they have white lips on a luscious purple body.

> The rarer the flowers are, the more trouble to keepe; the ordinary sorts on the contrary part will not be lost, doe what one will.

John Parkinson (1567–1650)

Soil and site Aquilegias like a moist but well-drained soil in sun or partial shade. The richer it is in humus the better your plants will be. Knockout flower stems can be as tall as 1m/3ft and carry more than a dozen flowers. **Propagation** Happy plants hybridize freely and self-seed profusely. Left to their own devices they generally revert to type in a few generations. The only guaranteed way to perpetuate named cultivars is to divide established clumps early in spring. The roots resent disturbance though and take a long time to recover however gently you prise them apart. Parkinson's advice of 1629 remains as fresh today as ever.

left: *Aquilegia* 'Winky'

brunnera macrophylla

Cultivation Large-leaved plants lose a lot of moisture to the air and generally prefer a deep moist soil. Some of them like bergenia and winter heliotrope have a waxy or shiny surface that reduces transpiration. Brunneras have rough leaves and require permanently moist soil if they are to thrive. Ensure that brunneras are always cool, shaded, sheltered and well watered.

Perfect planting Brunneras provide excellent balance around large plants with finely cut foliage or relatively small leaves. They are especially good around roses and Moutan peonies where evergreen ground covers can look too shiny and solid. Variegated forms are especially attractive in this context.

Propagation Brunneras will suffer if you try to divide them when in full leaf, so lift and replant them very early in spring or in autumn to increase your stock.

right: *Brunnera macrophylla* 'Hadspen Cream'

Siberian bugloss Horticultural jargon is convenient shorthand but it sometimes misrepresents a plant's full potential. Just as 'ground cover' too easily translates as 'useful but dull' so 'foliage plant' often means 'nice leaves, shame about the flowers'. 'Excellent as a cut flower' can be the most damning phrase of all, being short for 'excellent as a cut flower but a frightful mess in the garden'. So, how shall we categorize brunnera? Well, it has large, rough-textured heart-shaped leaves that are remarkably handsome, and there are some striking variegated forms, so it's definitely a foliage plant. Forming dense, generously arching clumps against which weeds don't stand a chance it makes excellent deciduous ground cover. Yet when the leaves are copiously topped off in mid and late spring with delicate sprays of bright blue forget-me-not-like flowers it becomes the tour de force of any border. If this superlative marriage of sense and sensibility does not qualify it as 'a good all-rounder', then quite simply what would?

The long-lasting flowers are carried in loose airy panicles 20cm/8in or so long on thin wiry stems. The total height is around 45cm/18in. The leaves are about 15cm/6in long by 10cm/4in wide at the time of flowering but new foliage assumes fuller, more rounded proportions as the year draws on. To keep plants looking perky well into autumn, scissor out any tired-looking leaves in mid summer and new ones will quickly grow to replace them.

Bog-standard *Brunnera macrophylla* has mid-green leaves and is the toughest of the lot. *B. m.* 'Betty Bowring' is a white-flowered form which I think rather misses the point. The leaves of *B. m.* 'Hadspen Cream' have irregular creamy-white borders on a light green ground with some interesting bright green splotches. *B. m.* 'Langtrees' is dark green with white spotting around the border. *B. m.* 'Variegata' is the most dashing of all with grey-green leaves so broadly edged creamy-white that some are almost albino; the flowers contrast brilliantly with the foliage and the whole plant is a real bobby-dazzler.

camellia

Recommended varieties With single red blooms in early spring and smooth, shiny leaves *Camellia japonica* is the most popular species; a great many stunning cultivars have been developed which flower at different times from winter onwards. *C. j.* 'Nobilissima' bears white peony-like flowers from late winter to mid spring. *C. j.* 'Coquettii' likes to keep you guessing. It has large deep red blooms in early and mid spring; they can be very double and formal looking, more relaxed and peony-like, or less double and more like anemones. One of the oldest cultivars, *C. j.* 'Tricolor' has crinkled foliage and semi-double flowers striped white, pink and red that appear in mid spring. The American-bred *C. j.* 'Cinderella' is a pale pink semi-double heavily suffused deep rose with white frilly edges to its crinkled petals; quite a beauty.

From early to late spring *C. j.* 'Ave Maria' has soft-pink double blooms with the crisp elegance of those oriental garnishes intricately carved from vegetables. *C. x williamsii* cultivars are hybrids of *C. japonica* and *C. saluenensis*, which tend to flower in mid and late spring. There are some especially attractive shapes and colours. *C. x w.* 'Jury's Yellow' has anemone-like white flowers with frilly scrunched up centres of titchy yellow petals. *C. x w.* 'E. G. Waterhouse' has generously sized double pink blooms that are somewhat cup-shaped and resemble English roses when young, then waterlilies when fully open. The single *C. x w.* 'Francis Hanger' has classically simple pure white petals around a prominent central mass of golden yellow stamens. *C. x w.* 'J. C. Williams' is similar in form but palest shell-pink in colour.

left: *Camellia japonica* 'Dixie Knight'; right: *Camellia x williamsii* 'E.G. Waterhouse'

Chinese rose · Japanese rose

Without even realizing it, you're probably no more than a few paces away from the best-loved, most ubiquitous camellia of all time. There might even be a pot of it by your side as you're reading these very words. Best watered from a boiling kettle, *Camellia sinensis* – the cup that cheers but not inebriates – is better known as tea.

Like rhododendrons, camellias are only a viable proposition if your soil is entirely free of lime, and preferably somewhat acid. However, they are a far better proposition for town gardens and for container cultivation because they are smaller and quicker to mature. Camellias are long lived but reach full stature at six to eight years of age; growth thereafter is very slow. A garden specimen won't swamp its neighbours, a pot-plant won't get itchy feet, and you won't be fagged with pruning.

Even in acid conditions camellias can develop the alarming symptoms usually associated with alkaline soil. First the leaves turn a sickly yellow, then they die. It all comes down to lack of humus. Always dig large planting holes for camellias and back-fill them generously with well-rotted compost and manure. This is a job you can only do once, so be sure to do it well. Mulch them with similar good stuff each autumn both to keep on enriching the soil and to build up a good layer of organic matter to reduce moisture-loss from the roots. Dry soil leads to bud drop.

Many tender camellia species are sold as houseplants and conservatory specimens. Plant them outdoors when they've grown too large and they'll die of cold. Sadly, these give garden varieties a bad name when in fact (and quite contrary to popular belief) they rank amongst the hardiest of evergreen shrubs. As early as 1827 Joseph Harrison, gardener at Wortley Hall in Yorkshire, described the camellia as hardier even than the laurel in a paper for the Royal Horticultural Society. No one ever believes this, and it's easy to see why: the leaves might be as tough as shoe-leather but the flowers are often spoilt by frost. They needn't be, the secret lies in thoughtful positioning. Frozen flowers and buds can blacken and die if they thaw out too quickly. The colder your climate, the more important it is to avoid direct morning sunshine on *any* winter- or early spring-flowering plant. Plant camellias where they're shaded until lunchtime and sheltered from drying winds.

Now you know how straightforward they are to grow, I hope you've worked up a thirst for one of your own. Why not choose a camellia for your garden today?

ceanothus

Pruning On evergreens cut all the previous season's growth back by half once flowering is over. This summer's woody growth will carry next spring's flowers. Don't be timid, pruning must commence the year after planting. If a plant is leggy when you buy it, prune it when you plant it (cruel = kind, lazy = you'll be sorry).

Propagation Take heeled, semi-ripe cuttings of evergreen varieties in mid to late summer. Better still, buy yourself a deciduous variety.

Feeding Since they expend a lot of energy blooming their hearts out in springtime, reward them in the autumn with a generous mulch of well-rotted garden compost.

In full bloom these fantastic shrubs are a heaving, bubbling mass of glorious rich blue froth.

California lilac There are about 55 species of this mainly western North American and Mexican shrub. They hybridize freely so there are a great many more cultivated varieties to choose from. This needn't be confusing, because for gardening purposes they fall neatly into two camps. The evergreens begin flowering in mid to late spring; they are a little tender and are best grown against a sunny wall sheltered from cold winds. Deciduous varieties are hardier and bloom from mid summer to autumn; they can be safely grown in the open.

As you can imagine they all thrive in hot and arid situations which remind them of their native homelands. Once they have settled in they are excellent shrubs for gardeners who have neither the time nor the inclination for watering. However, there are a couple of points to bear in mind if your chosen cultivar is to be a really fine specimen.

Firstly, although ceanothus are tolerant of lime, they can only put up with really thin chalky soil for a year or two before their leaves turn an unhealthy chlorotic yellow. Postpone this indefinitely by potting out your treasure in a broad deep planting hole heavily enriched with good garden compost and well-rotted manure. Generous planting is always a wise future investment.

Secondly, it is important to prune ceanothus right from the outset if they are to look good, live long and prosper. Rapid height comes at the expense of substance. Untrained specimens get leggy at the base with age. Renovation pruning to rectify this rarely works since new growth does not break easily from old wood. Tired, ugly plants, I'm afraid, are best dug up, chucked out then replaced with something new.

The tiny flowerbuds of ceanothus are densely packed together either in longish panicles or in more rounded multi-branched clusters called cymes. These in turn are borne along the stems in profusion. The following evergreens all flower in spring. *Ceanothus* 'Cascade' has powder-blue panicles to 6cm/2½in long on gracefully arching stems that create a water-fall effect against walls. The conical honey-scented mid-blue panicles of *C. arboreus* 'Trewithen Blue' are up to 12cm/5in long. *C.* 'Blue Mound' has dark blue flowers in long 7cm/3in cymes; it is hummock forming and looks like an avalanche when grown against a wall. *C.* 'Concha' has round indigo cymes to 4cm/1½in across. *C. purpureus* has violet-blue to purple flowers in flattish cymes up to 4cm/1½in across.

left: *Ceanothus* 'Puget Blue'

Pruning and training After flowering thin out old and crowded branches on established free-standing bushes. Aim for a relaxed, natural look. Hedges only need clipping once a year; this annual late spring or early summer trim keeps things tidy and increases the flowering side-shoots, or spurs. Given the support of a wall, chaenomeles can be pruned very hard indeed to stimulate dense blossom cover. Cut back most of last season's end growth and all of the side growth to just two or three buds. The new wood that sprouts from these buds forms next spring's flower spurs. Plants pruned this way bloom even more profusely as the years roll by. Spur systems eventually become too congested so prune out a few of the oldest each year.

Propagation Take heeled cuttings in mid to late summer or, alternatively, layer low-lying stems in autumn.

Forcing Stems cut towards the end of winter will burst prematurely into bloom indoors.

chaenomeles

Flowering quince · Japanese quince · Japonica

For me, this hardy shrub epitomises springtime. It blooms continuously from the end of winter to the beginning of summer; the first flowers are carried proudly ahead of the leaves on naked branches; the final stragglers are tucked in shyly amongst the mid-green foliage. They are fully hardy but burst into bloom earlier if grown against a sunny wall. Hot summer sunshine guarantees a generous supply of attractive autumn fruits, doubling the plant's garden value.

Chaenomeles japonica is a low-growing shrub rarely exceeding 1m/3ft in height but generally achieving a spread of around 2m/6½ft. With only a very little formative training young specimens can be formed into a dwarf rustic hedge that has two seasons of interest and requires little ongoing maintenance. Depending on your standpoint, the odd extremely sharp thorn is either a curse or a blessing. Like fiery orange-red apple-blossom, the 4cm/1½in cup-shaped flowers each have five rounded petals and are borne singly or in clusters. The oval 5cm/2in long leaves are downy and toothed. The 2.5cm/1in

yellow fruits resemble crab-apples but they are clamped so tightly to the bush they are often indented by the branches. Rock hard even when fully ripe, they make a long-lasting slightly comical display. Japanese quinces are heavily fragrant and can be used for scenting clothes and linen. Only with a great deal of patience can they be used for cooking. Just in case you're wondering the culinary quince, *Cydonia oblonga*, is in an entirely different genus. It has larger, pale pink flowers in early summer and furry pear-shaped fruit about 12cm/5in long in autumn.

The best-known flowering quince is the erect *Chaenomeles speciosa*, which can reach a height of 2m/6ft6in in open ground, more if wall trained. It has 5cm/2in diameter flowers and there are many different varieties: *C. s.* 'Nivalis' and *C. s.* 'Snow' have white blossom; *C. s.* 'Moerloosei' is white flushed pink; *C. s.* 'Falconnet Charlet' has double salmon-pink blossom; *C. s.* 'Simonii' has an almost prostrate habit and double, dark crimson flowers.

C. x superba hybrids have *C. japonica* and *C. speciosa* varieties as parents. They form rounded shrubs to about 1.5m/5ft and cover the same colour range as *C. speciosa*.

Planting Any fertile, moist, but well-drained soil will do nicely. *Clematis armandii* can attain a height of 6m/20ft and a spread of around 3m/10ft so its water demands can be high. The soil immediately at the foot of a wall can be very dry so plant your clematis at least 30cm/12in away (more if you dare) and lean it towards the brickwork with a cane. This looks odd until the plant is established but pays huge dividends in terms of rapid growth and low long-term maintenance.

Pruning and training This clematis climbs both by training and by sending out tendrils. Demarcate its territory with a few discreet horizontal wires or with an ornamental trellis. Late in a plant's first spring encourage generous branching from the base by cutting all stems back to buds about 30cm/12in from the ground. The second spring cut all stems back to about 1m/3ft. Thereafter leave the plant alone except to prune out dead or damaged stems or to keep things within bounds once flowering is over.

clematis armandii

Clematis armandii Native to central and southern China, this popular evergreen clematis was brought to the West in 1900 by Ernest Henry Wilson and named for the French missionary and plant collector Père Armand David. Like the winter-flowering *Clematis cirrhosa*, *C. armandii* is not fully hardy but will invariably succeed against a sheltered sunny wall. In the unfortunate event of a plant failing under really adverse weather conditions during its first or second winter, buy another and try again. Once a plant is well established, it will regrow again from the base if cut to the ground by frost. Frost, in fact, is much less of a menace than desiccating winter winds, which can shrivel the foliage and scorch the flowerbuds. If faced with the choice of a sunny yet exposed site or a shady but sheltered corner, shelter should always be the deciding factor when positioning this plant. All other things being equal, shade produces larger lusher leaves that bring a year-round subtropical element to the garden. Ample sunshine brings far more flowers from early to mid spring.

The leaves of this clematis are composed of three oval to lance-shaped leaflets each up to 15cm/6in long. They are a glossy dark green on top, bluish beneath, leathery in texture and prominently veined. Besides providing perfect cover for less-than-perfect walls and fences, the vines make excellent cut-flower foliage and create a luxurious effect spilling out of a vase.

C. armandii's flowers are comprised of four to six narrow, pure white petals – botanically these are tepals, there being no real distinction in clematis between petals and sepals. The blooms are around 5cm/2in across and are carried in profusion on all stems two years old or more. They hang in clusters from stalks in the leaf joints.

The flowers of all varieties have a vanilla and hawthorn fragrance. *C. a.* 'Apple Blossom' has rounded tepals forming open, cup-shaped blooms tinged with pink. *C. a.* 'Jeffries' has pure white flowers and narrower leaves than the type; it occasionally repeat flowers in summer. *C. a.* 'Snowdrift' has narrow pointed tepals that give blooms the look of snowflakes.

convallaria majalis

Planting If at first you don't succeed, try, try again. Lily-of-the-valley has a mind of its own and you might have to experiment with several different sites before finding one that is just right. The best kind of soil seems to be moist, moderately fertile, humus rich and leafy or open-textured. Heavy clay needs a lot of compost and grit adding before it can become a viable home.

Propagation Lift and carefully divide established clumps in autumn. Replant the rhizomes about 2.5cm/1in deep and tamp the earth down firmly. If we're talking swathes rather than clumps then lift whole sods with a spade or fork and transplant them to where they are needed.

> The Wood Lillie or Lillie of the Valley is a flower mervallous sweete, flourishing especially in the springtime and growing properly in woods.

Thomas Hyll (fl. 1540s–1570s)

Lily-of-the-valley In the Victorian Language of Flowers lily-of-the-valley signifies the Return of Happiness. In Norse mythology it is the flower of Ostara, goddess of the dawn. It is also the national flower of Finland. This northern European native is an extremely cold-tolerant species capable of withstanding winter temperatures below -20°C/-4°F. Hardy enough for anywhere then – but not easy for everyone to grow. It only really flourishes in sites that are cool and shady all year round, so it is more or less doomed to failure in southerly latitudes. This is a salutary reminder that hot sunny gardens don't have all the best plants. The softly shiny lance-shaped leaves arise from thongy underground rhizomes in early to mid spring and are closely followed by arching racemes of tight green buds. These open in late spring into sensuously fragrant white, waxy, rounded bell-shaped flowers. Adjectives just can't do justice to the sweet, sharp scent: lily-of-the-valley, I'm afraid, is the only possible description. The fruits are little red berries and come to prominence in autumn just before the leaves die away.

Plants aren't always easy to establish, but once they are happy they spread quickly by means of their creeping, branching rhizomes and can colonize large areas in just a few years. Lily-of-the-valley makes stylish ground cover in the wilder, woodland sort of garden and under shrubs in large, generously planted mixed borders. In dainty little flower gardens it can soon become a menace. If you're worried about an invasion try a spot of tactical planting. A clump or two will be happy in the shade at the back of a sunny border but if they spread anywhere it'll be into the relative coolness of your neighbour's garden. This is only fair practice if you suffer from encroaching weeds.

Convallaria majalis 'Albostriata' has leaves with longitudinal stripes of creamy-yellow but the flowers are slightly smaller than in the species. At 30cm/12in or so tall, *C. m.* 'Fortin's Giant' is one third as tall again and has broader leaves and larger blooms that open a little later. *C. m.* var. *rosea* has unutterably foul pale mauve-pink flowers; pray to Ostara for a thunderbolt if your neighbour grows it.

corydalis flexuosa

Blue fumitory True blue flowers are rarities prized for the unique shot of colour they inject into a garden. At first sight it seems a common enough hue but close inspection reveals otherwise: most 'blue' flowers contain more than a touch of red pigment and veer towards purple on the spectrum. For intellectual convenience we use the word to describe any colour in nature from aquamarine to violet but we rarely encounter it pure and uncut outside a paint chart. When we do, we recognize instinctively that we're in the presence of something special. Why else would we get such a huge emotional buzz on seeing blue morning glories, ceanothus and Himalayan poppies for the first time? Beware. Blue flowers are addictive.

Corydalis flexuosa was introduced to horticulture as recently as 1989 from Sichuan Province in China. This uncannily beautiful plant still holds novelty value for collectors yet is easy to cultivate and lies well within every gardener's grasp.

Corydalis comes from the Greek for lark, a reference to the tapering spurs that link the greater part of all flowers in the genus and which (fancifully) resemble the backward projection on a lark's foot. In *C. flexuosa* the tubular 2.5 cm/1 in long flowers are held prettily in loose but generous clusters on thin but succulent stems above glaucous green foliage, like a fleshier version of maidenhair fern. Individual plants have a height and spread of around 30 cm/12 in. For me the dynamic shape of the flowers is a vital part of their appeal, it imparts a very real sense of movement giving the impression of darting shoals of electric blue minnows. Unfortunately slugs and snails have reasons of their own for finding the plant attractive, the fresh juicy leaves (prosaically) resembling lunch.

In the cool woodland terrain of its homeland *C. flexuosa* is a natural companion to the stately ostrich or shuttlecock fern *Matteuccia struthiopteris* and in gardens it associates well with all shade-loving foliage plants and is especially attractive interplanted with Bowles' golden grass *Milium effusum* 'Aureum'. Although it makes exquisite underplanting for deciduous shrubs it is soon defeated by heavily rooted trees – for that job send in yellow-flowering stalwart *C. lutea*, which can even colonize walls and will naturalize happily if left to self-seed.

Soil and site Dappled shade is essential, as is an open-textured, moist, but well-drained soil with more than its fair share of humus. A large planting hole generously enriched with leaf mould and grit will get plants off to a flying start, while a handful of grit sprinkled on the soil surface closes the restaurant door on slimy freeloaders.

Care and propagation Deadheading can extend the flowering season from late spring well into summer. The plant becomes dormant until autumn when older clumps should be lifted and divided if their vigour is to be maintained. From late autumn onwards young leaves brave the elements to enliven the winter garden and muster forces for the big spring display.

Care and cultivation Plant crocus bulbs in autumn three times as deep as they are round, about 7cm/3in below ground level. On heavy clay mix some grit into the soil to improve drainage and prevent rotting. How far apart they go is down to you. Dense planting gives instant impact; wider spacing is more economical. Over time, small clumps grow larger and well-spaced drifts fill in nicely. Squirrels and mice love to eat the bulbs – if you find this a problem, grow your crocuses in the lawn where they're much harder to dig up.

Ever wondered...? Creepy-crawlies are especially attracted to yellow flowers, which is why sticky fly-papers are invariably this colour. When birds start pecking crocuses to bits they always start with the yellow ones because they serve bigger portions of grub.

A word to the wise I don't care how big and cheap they are, mixed bags of differently coloured crocuses are never a bargain. However beautifully you arrange the bulbs, the results look as if someone has tipped over a tin of old sweet wrappers. Instead, plant contrasting drifts in different shades and colours – the results look stunning.

crocus tommasinianus

Crocus Every autumn garden centres and D.I.Y. stores sell crocuses in string bags, supermarkets sell them in cardboard boxes, gift shops sell them in holey terracotta clogs and dinky wee animals. Everybody buys them and every spring, lawns, flowerbeds, window boxes and flowerpots are full of crocuses. I wouldn't have it any other way. But...

Wouldn't it be nice if they didn't all come out at once? Thanks to hard-working Dutch bulb growers one species in particular, *Crocus vernus*, has become so widely available it has more or less eclipsed the rest. Selective breeding has produced a wide assortment of hybrids and cultivars that are hardy, happy in poor soil and flower year after year each spring. All at the same time. Stagger the season with *C. tommasinianus* and you'll stagger passers-by too because it starts into bloom at the end of winter, easily a month before *C. vernus* pokes its head above ground.

There are about 80 species in the genus and not all of them are easy to grow. *C. tommasinianus*, however, thrives in precisely the same conditions as *C. vernus*. It is equally suitable for naturalizing in grass. It increases just as freely by offsets and even more freely by seed. If anything, it is more elegant in flower as the petals are generally narrower and more pointed. The only difficulty in growing *C. tommasinianus* lies in tracking down a supplier. The species ranges in colour from pale mauve to lilac; in *C. t.* var. *pictus* the outer petals have darker tips; *C. t.* f. *albus* is pure white; *C. t.* var. *roseus* is rose-pink. *C. t.* 'Whitewell Purple' has reddish-purple petals that are silver-mauve on the inside; *C. t.* 'Barr's Purple' is purple inside, silvery outside. *C. t.* 'Ruby Giant' is bigger than the rest and forms impressive clumps but doesn't set seed; the rounded beetroot-red petals suggest it is a hybrid with *C. vernus*. Happy hunting!

dicentra spectabilis

Bleeding heart · ladies' lockets With its bright fern-like foliage, arching red stems and rows of exquisitely formed late spring flowers, you'd expect this gem to be in every garden. Misuse and abuse has led to its decline. There's nothing new in this. *Dicentra spectabilis* was first brought to the West from Siberia in 1810 but it died out pretty quickly. Robert Fortune reintroduced it in 1846 from a grotto garden on the Japanese island of Chusan. It became so popular that by 1878 Robert Thompson wrote in *The Gardener's Assistant* that 'its gracefully drooping spikes of heart-shaped pink flowers have become so familiar to many as wallpaper pattern, that further description will be needless.' What can we do to bring it back into favour?

A quick biology lesson. A plant grows leaves to turn sunshine into food by the process of photosynthesis. The sugars formed give it the energy to grow larger so it can flower and set seed. In perennials some of the products of photosynthesis go to their roots to be stored in the form of starch. These plants draw on their food reserves to start into growth again the following year after a period of dormancy.

A quick ecology lesson. Herbaceous perennials from deciduous woodlands are earlier to send up leaves and earlier to flower than plants from more open habitats. As summer reaches its height, woodlanders are enveloped on all sides by the thickening leaf canopy of surrounding trees and shrubs, that progressively excludes light. The coolness and the darkness send these forest-floor dwellers into the decline and dormancy which in most garden plants is associated with the onset of autumn.

Well, waddya know? If you apply conventional spacing wisdom when growing ladies' lockets in a border, it will suffer from too much exposure as summer draws on and you will suffer the embarrassment of a gaping great hole in your late summer display. Neither of you will be happy. Either the plant will die or you will hoick it out in disgust. Halt this decline by shoving it slap-bang up against any large-leaved sun-loving perennial. The plant will thrive and you will get a great spring show every year with no subsequent summer gap. Remarkably simple really!

> The white variety, too seldom seen, is also very beautiful when associated with the pink kind. *The Garden* 1874

Soil Really open-textured, leafy, humus-rich soil works wonders and will produce specimens around 1m/3ft tall. Ordinary garden loam is fertile enough but the consistency isn't quite right; leaf mould or cocoa-husks make excellent conditioners. A neutral-to-alkaline pH is preferred, so if your soil is acid I suggest you plant ladies' lockets next to *Crambe cordifolia* – all will be revealed later (p.92)...

Propagation Divide the fleshy rhizomatous roots early in spring or, better still, after the leaves die down in summer but only if this doesn't disturb surrounding plants.

doronicum orientale

Perfect planting It is tempting to put early-flowering stunners like leopard's bane towards the front of a border so you can admire them at close quarters. Don't. They're perfectly visible towards the middle or back where it's easier to provide them with summer shade and where their early autumn absence won't be noted. Summer borders are usually arranged in ascending tiers with the small plants at the front and the large ones at the back so that every flower can be seen in full-on glory. In the sparser spring border there's far less competition for your attention and you get more of an aerial view, so the trick is to spread star plants about between winter-flowering shrubs, evergreen or early ground cover, and stands of bulbs. This is why you can plant titchy little things like lily-of-the-valley (p.59) right at the back yet still get the full benefit.

Propagation Elementary, my dear Watson. Divide in autumn or very early in spring.

These big yellow daisies on strong, tall stems look as though they've travelled back in a time machine from summer.

Leopard's bane This is a native of south-eastern Europe, Asia Minor and the Caucasus where it is found on the edges of mountainous woodland and in scrub. What would Sherlock Holmes infer from this? Like *Dicentra spectabilis* it appears early, in mid to late spring, then fades into obscurity in mid summer. In the garden leopard's bane prefers a drier, sandier loam than ladies' lockets, in fact its roots are prone to rot in soils that are too moist and rich in humus. It is accustomed to summer shade and likes to spend its retirement in the close company of later-flowering leafy perennials and under the arching branches of shrubs. Early to flower; warm native climate; rocky terrain; woodland setting. The clues were all there.

The mid-green leaves of *Doronicum orientale* are long and pointed with heart-shaped bases where they meet the flowering stem. The ones close to the ground are up to 10cm/4in long;

those higher up the flower stems are shorter and smaller, truly heart-shaped. All the leaves have scalloped edges. Arising from slowly creeping rhizomes, the stems reach a height of 50–60cm/20–24in and each one is tipped with a bright rayed yellow 2.5–5cm/1–2in flower like a child's drawing of a daisy. With their long stems and cheerful blooms it is easy to see why doronicums are grown commercially for use by florists.

D. orientale 'Goldcut' has considerably stiffer stems and larger blooms then the species, making it an excellent cut flower. The stems of *D. o.* 'Magnificum' on the other hand branch sparingly so you get several blooms to a stalk and fuller-looking vases. *D.* 'Finesse' is especially delicate-looking as the rays are curled along their length into slender quills. *D.* 'Frühlingspracht' has smaller sturdy double flowers; *D.* 'Gerhard' is a lemon-yellow double with a greenish centre.

erysimum 'bowles' mauve'

Perennial wallflower *The* wallflower is *Erysimum cheiri* with its richly fragrant yellow, orange or blood-red blooms. For best results plants are grown from seed each year then transplanted to their final positions in autumn. Because they flower in mid to late spring they are often used in association with tulips and forget-me-nots in large formal bedding schemes, which look and smell fantastic. As the show draws to a close the whole lot are then chucked out as fit for nothing and replaced with something else for summer. While I can admire this approach in the appropriate setting, I really can't be fagged with it myself. However, the genus *Erysimum* has more than 80 species and there are some very useful hybrids. For the small, low-maintenance garden the wallflower of choice has got to be *E.* 'Bowles' Mauve'. It lives for years, it is fully hardy and evergreen, it thrives in poor dry soil on exposed and windy sites, it is excellent by the sea and *it is never out of flower*. All in all, it's one great big can of instant whup-ass.

In fact, *E. cheiri* is an evergreen perennial too, but gardeners treat it as they do because it is very short lived. It soon grows lanky, and it flowers less well as it ages. *E.* 'Bowles' Mauve' on the other hand, is tough, shrubby, and grows more and more floriferous. The tightly packed stems on a well-kept specimen are fully decked with narrow lance-shaped cabbage-blue leaves and form a solid dome of foliage around 45cm/18in high. Flat clusters of buds at the stem tips become more rounded as they open and gradually elongate to 30cm/12in racemes of four-petalled mauve flowers about 1.5cm/³⁄₄in across. Once a raceme is spent, it will have carried somewhere in the region of 70 individual blooms.

The flower and foliage colours of *E.* 'Bowles' Mauve' set each other off perfectly but the plant does have one shortcoming – there is no scent to speak of. The smaller, yellow *E.* 'Walberton's Fragrant Sunshine', which holds its flowers closer to its chest, rectifies this, but before you plant it, do remember that the garden is never short of yellow in spring.

Family background Erysimums belong to the Cruciferae family which includes the genera *Brassica* (cabbage), *Rorippa* (watercress) and *Wasabia* (wasabe). They all have that distinctive school-greens sulphurous smell when crushed. The flowers are always cruciform, that is, four-petalled.

A dash of lime Crucifers grow best in alkaline or chalky soil. If your soil is acidic or neutral, raise the pH by adding a shake of Dolomitic limestone when planting ornamentals such as aubrieta, crambe and stocks. Plants are sturdier and longer-lived in dryish, well-drained soils that *aren't* enriched with humus.

Dead-heading The main flowering period is from late winter to summer. However if you trim back the stems a little in mid summer to clear away all the spent racemes, you'll stimulate a second lighter flush of flowers that will last into wintertime.

Propagation *Erysimum* 'Bowles' Mauve' is sterile so doesn't set seed. Heeled cuttings taken in mid to late summer root easily and can be planted straight into the garden.

Frogspawn bush · spurge This is just one of at least two thousand other spurges in a vast genus. Species range from annuals to perennials, cactus-like succulents to shrubs. The most widely recognized euphorbia is the tender *E. pulcherrima*, or poinsettia, and it will be useful to focus on this for a moment. The 'flower' isn't what it seems. Those red 'petals' aren't petals but bracts, which are leaf-like structures at the base of the real flower stalks. The real flowers are those tiny yellow thingummies clustered in the middle. Zooming in on hardy *E. characias*, yellow-green bracts form cups called cyathia. These hold several pale green stamens each equivalent to a male flower, and one stalked ovary equivalent to a female. A ring of purplish nectar-secreting glands surrounds these flowers. To pull back a little now, the cyathia are clustered at the end of long stalks in dense oval cymes. These giant inflorescences easily reach lengths of 30cm/12in or so.

When you step back to admire the whole plant it is a truly magnificent sight. Stems reach a height of 1–1.5m/3–5ft; they are carried in a generous clump arising from a woody base so a mature stand can be a good metre or so across. Usually around 15–20cm/6–8in long, the evergreen glaucous leaves are narrow and pointed. They are arranged in dense spirals up the stalks. Older stems become bare at the base and resemble giant loo-brushes.

The inflorescences are carried on the previous season's shoots and open slowly from late winter to the end of spring. They remain in excellent condition till mid autumn. *E. c.* subsp. *characias* 'Blue Hills' has blue-green leaves and forms a compact 1m/3ft mound when mature. *E. c.* subsp. *c.* 'Humpty Dumpty' has glossy dark brown cyathia. *E. c.* subsp. *wulfenii* has cymes which are shorter and more spherical and also differs in having yellow nectaries in brighter cyathia; it has more impact from afar but less of the frogspawn effect close-up. An outstanding cultivar is *E. c.* subsp. *w.* 'Purple and Gold' whose leaves are deep purple when young.

E. characias comes from the western Mediterranean but it is reliably hardy given a light, well-drained soil in full sun. Specimens in rich moist soil wear themselves out too quickly and their lush growth is susceptible to frost damage in winter. All spurges have poisonous thick white sap that is a skin irritant: plant them a good arm's length from any pathway. Euphorbia leaves are toxic to fish, so keep them well away from poolsides. Cut flowering shoots back to ground level in autumn. The remaining growth from the current season will flower in spring.

euphorbia characias

Propagation Take pencil-length cuttings of stem bases in late spring. To prevent the sap bleeding excessively, dip the cut ends lickety-split in warm water before potting up.

Good companions *Euphorbia characias* and *Erysimum* 'Bowles' Mauve' (opposite) set each other off beautifully and thrive in poor dry sites where many plants fail. Repeat the effect in miniature with *E. myrsinites* tumbling over walls beside aubretia.

Treat 'em mean and keep 'em keen. These towering plumes of blue-green foliage tipped with massive Chartreuse flowerheads thrive on neglect.

fritillaria imperialis

Invest in the future A good plump bulb won't stay that way for long unless you nourish it well. The first year a crown imperial flowers, all credit should go to your supplier. In subsequent years, the glory is all yours. Or the shame. Usually, I'm afraid, it's the latter. Specimens just fade away, never to reappear. These plants are gross feeders and diminishing returns will soon set in unless the ground is really well enriched with compost and manure. Potassium promotes healthy flower growth so a little rock potash or wood ash mixed into the soil at planting time won't go amiss either, and neither will a generous mulch each autumn. Phew!

Dividends Bulbs need lifting and replanting with fresh mulch and potash every four years or so. Do this when they go dormant in summer. It reinvigorates old plants and provides you with baby bulbs to put elsewhere.

Limited partners All this mulching and digging means you can't plant crown imperials under permanent groundcover or close to large perennials whose roots you might damage. Close up the gap they leave behind in mid summer with self-seeding annuals such as pot marigolds (*Calendula officinalis*), love-in-a-mist (*Nigella damascena*) or most dramatic of all, Himalayan balsam (*Impatiens glandulifera*, p.97).

In the bottom of each of these bels there is placed six drops of most cleare shining sweet water, in taste like sugar, resembling in show faire orient pearles; the which drops if you take away, there do immediately appeare the like.

John Gerard (1545–1612)

Crown imperial Native to Turkey, Iran, Afghanistan and Pakistan, this is one of the oldest known cultivated ornamental plants and surely still the most achingly beautiful. The large bulbs go into rapid growth in early spring, thick sturdy green stems quickly shoot up bearing whorls of glossy, narrow 10–20cm/4–8in mid-green leaves for their first 50cm/20in. Atop the second half of the stem, which is stained purplish-brown, there appear up to eight nodding, bell-shaped, tulip-sized flowers surmounted by a pineapple-like headdress of leafy green bracts. I would be lying if I said it was easy to grow, but I would be crazy to say it isn't worth all the effort it takes. Crown imperials don't require round-the-clock nursing care, they just needs a little bit of love and attention once in a while. As do we all.

The flattish bulbs, which give off a suspiciously foxy odour when handled, are 10cm/4in in diameter and best put in the soil as soon as possible after purchase in summer. A planting hole 30cm/12in deep with the bottom well forked over with compost and manure is about right.

There are some stunning varieties. *Fritillaria imperialis* 'Lutea' is a bright yellow; the gorgeous *F. i.* 'Maxima Lutea' is a taller and larger-flowered form. *F. i.* 'Sulpherino' has soft tangerine blooms veined in purple with yellow margins. *F. i.* 'The Premier' is orange with purple veining. *F. i.* 'Argentovariegata' is less vigorous with rusty orange flowers and creamy-white edged foliage, the leaves and bracts of *F. i.* 'Aureomarginata' are edged butter yellow. *F. i.* 'Rubra' has dark burnt-orange flowers with purple veins; *F. i.* 'Rubra Maxima' is darker still. *F. i.* 'Prolifera', or 'Crown upon Crown', has two whorls of orange-red flowers, one upon another.

Whatever form you choose, each petal has a prominent white nectary at the base which attracts bees and wasps in droves and ensures pollination of the blooms. When your guests have had their fill I suggest you pinch out each flower as it fades. A plant can devote a lot of energy to seed production which would arguably be better directed into fattening up the bulb ready for next year's show. Propagation from seed is too tedious for words; happy bulbs produce offsets all by themselves.

Cultivation Damp but well-drained leafy soil and a little light shade are all the home comforts these plants require. Now for the bad news: they're a little frost tender. In a warm and sheltered site this needn't be a problem. Gardeners in very cold climates can plant *Iris confusa* in pots, which can be temporarily sheltered in a shed or garage during severe winter cold spells.

Propagation Lift and divide congested clumps in late summer or early autumn. Try to spread out the rhizomes as you replant them to accentuate the airy and languid habit of the developing stems and leaves.

Designing with plants Western gardens can be given an oriental touch without any gimmicky hard-landscaping if they're planted evocatively. Japanese maples (*Acer palmatum*, p.118), camellias (p.54), *Clematis armandii* (p.58), hostas (*Hosta plantaginea*, p.95), Himalayan honeysuckle (*Leycesteria formosa*, p.139), peonies (*Paeonia suffruticosa* p.74), Chinese lanterns (*Physalis alkekengi*, p.142) and wisteria (p.114) all have the right look.

iris confusa

Flat bamboo orchid This graceful evergreen makes a year-round architectural statement so breathtaking that most of us would grow it for the habit and foliage alone. With its delicate display of mid spring flowers it stops you dead in your tracks. This is an intriguing plant that people can't help but be drawn to. On seeing it for the first time it is easier to describe in terms of what it isn't rather than to commit yourself to saying what it is.

The tall segmented stems have prominent nodes where each section joins the next. Arching out from each node is a long strappy pointed leaf. These leaves sprout from alternate sides right the way up to the top and push each successive segment slightly out of alignment with its predecessor. This gives full-grown stems a gently zig-zagging outline. Clumps resemble stands of green bamboo and look as if they're from a Chinese ink and brush painting. The effect is of bamboo yet the plant is clearly not woody and the stems are, in fact, flat not round.

At the top of each 60–80cm/24–32in stem is a fan of about a dozen leaves from which 20–30cm/8–12in long wiry flower stalks emerge in spring. These carry airy branching sprays of elegant blooms. There are three to five flowers per spray, and four to six sprays per stalk. This means each stalk can carry around 30 flowers! They don't all open at once, but plants at this stage are remarkably orchid-like yet stand a whopping 1m/3ft or more tall. Quite a sight.

Close up, the flowers give the full picture. They are 4–5cm/1½–2in across and quite definitely irises. With petals the colours of willow-pattern pottery, the falls have a central yellow crest. See this plant once and you're forever smitten.

It's an iris Jim, but not as we know it.

lunaria annua

Honesty · moonwort · silver dollar · satin flower

No gardener should be without this. It is an attractive annual, biennial or short-lived perennial with bright foliage and cheerful flowers in late spring and early summer. It also provides attractive pearly seedheads for indoor displays. Most important of all, it is one of those prolific self-seeders which can be relied upon to plug the inevitable seasonal gaps that appear in every herbaceous border.

At full height honesty stands around 1m/3ft tall. Its heart-shaped mid-green leaves are coarsely toothed and up to about 15cm/6in long. The fragrant 1cm/½in diameter cruciform mauve to pink flowers are borne in loose clusters on short stems arising from the leaf axils. Some plants have very washed-out colouring so it's worth selecting a good, named form. *Lunaria annua* 'Munstead Purple' has rich reddish-purple blooms. *L. a.* var. *atrococcinea* is rose-magenta. *L. a. variegata* has leaves margined creamy-white. *L. a.* var. *albiflora* has pure white flowers, while the white blooms of *L. a.* 'Alba Variegata' are partnered by leaves with heavily variegated margins. This last cultivar is truly outstanding; variegation is so bold in young plants that the uppermost leaves are almost pure glistening white, but green gets the better of them with age.

Purple honesty in its first flush is a beautiful contrast in form and colour to late-blooming yellow daffodils. The later flowers nicely fill out the burgeoning border then are gone by mid summer. *L. a.* 'Alba Variegata' with its stunning light-reflecting foliage not only brightens dark corners long before the flowers appear, but continues to do so after they have gone.

To use the dollar- or old-penny-sized seedpods in dried flower arrangements, cut the stems as long as possible once the pods are fully formed and beginning to harden. Hang them upside down to dry in a cool, well-ventilated place. After a few weeks the dry outer scales are easily removed with thumb and forefinger to reveal the translucent moons, according to Gerard 'like white satten newly cut from the peece', honestly displaying their flat black seeds. This dusty job is best done outdoors.

Sowing and growing This couldn't be simpler. Plants left *in situ* will sort themselves out. After preparing stems for indoors scatter the seedy detritus around the garden yourself. Do this straightaway in late summer, early in spring, or half and half. Whatever you do, seedlings will pop up in autumn *and* in spring so at any one time you will have plants in different stages of growth. Variegated forms are more striking in spring if they have germinated in autumn.

Transplanting and thinning Be ruthless and be purposeful. When you cut down late summer-flowering perennials in autumn fill what would otherwise be a springtime gap by planting clusters of decent-sized honesty seedlings bang up against them. Only hoe out or give away surplus youngsters when you're really sure you won't be needing them. As flowering declines, feel free to hoick out honesty to make room for neighbouring plants on the up and up. The forget-me-not (*Myosotis sylvatica*) is a smaller early-flowering self-seeder to use in this way.

Scents and sensibility The fetid aroma of skunk cabbage comes from indole, a substance here secreted by the spathe but found widely throughout nature. A high concentration is redolent of decay; in flowers it acts as a lure to pollinating flies. It is potent stuff and in too great a quantity is utterly repellent to humans but, like its animal equivalent scatol, which is found in civet and used in perfumery, minute doses are devastatingly attractive. Indole is reminiscent of warm human flesh and gives us a subliminal sexual thrill. This is why we find musky perfumes and flowers like hyacinths, lilies and tuberoses so alluring. Plants with animal overtones add ripeness and substance to the delicate floral notes in a garden. Use them when you can, if not for their individual bouquet then for your fuller sensual pleasure. It must be acknowledged that the musky scent of box, elder, flowering currants (p.79), hawthorn (p.25), privet and rowan trees all contribute to the sensuality of your garden.

left: *Lysichiton camtschatcensis*

lysichiton

Bog arum · skunk cabbage If you're bowled over by the bog arum's enormous 45cm/18in early spring flowers, you'll be knocked out by its subsequent 1m/3ft high banana-like leaves, which remain lush and green till autumn. Some of the most spectacular plants in the world come from permanently damp habitats – never threatened by drought, they can grow to simply enormous proportions. This semi-aquatic stunner's unique selling point to gardeners is that it's totally tropical-looking yet fully hardy in temperate climates; the downside is that only naturally occurring wet spots really suit it. Let's face it, you've either got a boggy streamside with rich, deep soil or you haven't. If you have, get digging and why not take the opportunity to put in some candelabra primulas at the same time.

The north-east Asian *Lysichiton camtschatcensis* is found predominantly in Japan and Kamchatka, where it forms large colonies in marshlands and alongside watercourses. The generic name comes from the Greek *lysis*, a loosening, and *chiton*, a cloak or tunic. It refers to the gradual unfurling of the white spathe, or sheath, to reveal the central club-like green spadix. These huge waxy blooms arise straight out of the muddy ground in pristine condition from large spreading rhizomes just below the surface. They have an attractive light, sweet scent with a musky backnote.

Skunk cabbage, the bog arum's North American counterpart grows even in the inhospitable climate of Alaska, concrete proof of the plant's extreme hardiness. It has bright buttercup yellow flowers and is a little larger and more vigorous. (Technically, the spathe is a coloured bract and the real flowers are the hundreds of greeny-yellow nubbins around the top of the spadix but hey, broad brush-stroke terms are in order here.) Its malodorous nickname is well earned: on a warm still day the surrounding air reeks of school greens and frightened skunk. Definitely a plant for the far side of your lake, m'lud.

magnolia stellata

Star magnolia With the exception of Moutan peonies, magnolias have the largest flowers you will ever find on a tree or shrub. It is tempting, but unwise, to choose one by plumping for the biggest-blooming specimen you can find. The flowers of the much coveted *Magnolia grandiflora*, for example, can be up to 25cm/10in across; unfortunately, trees can take up to ten years before putting on even a scanty summer show and they reach a galumphing 8m/26ft or so on maturity. *M. stellata*, on the other hand, need never exceed a height of 2.5m/8ft and bears copious 7–10cm/3–4in pure white blooms in early springtime within a year or two of planting.

In dry soil this Japanese streamside native quickly assumes an erect tree-like habit; given the moister conditions it prefers, it forms a broadly spreading multi-stemmed shrub. The bark on young stems smells pleasantly musky. The demurely scented many-petalled flowers open from silky felt-covered buds into the gleaming stars which give the plant its name. They are borne in succession from the end of winter to the middle of spring and the petals of older blooms drop attractively after attaining their full spread. The 5–10cm/2–4in leaves only emerge in late spring as flowering fades; they are a fresh light green and give a little yellow autumn colour. The only real competition for *M. stellata* comes from either the Chinese yulan, *M. denudata*, which has far fewer but much larger flowers shaped like waterlilies, or *M. liliiflora* whose tulip-like flowers open from slender wine-red buds very late in spring and so rarely suffer frost damage. Both of these form somewhat larger trees though.

M. stellata has many attractive varieties. *M. s.* 'Waterlily' doesn't resemble a waterlily at all but has more petals and larger flowers than the type. *M. s.* 'Chrysanthemiflora' lives up to its name with many shell pink petals in loose pom-pom blooms. The floriferous *M. s.* 'Jane Platt' is probably the deepest pink of all the cultivars and one of the most heavily petalled. For style, impact and length of flowering it takes an awful lot of beating.

Soil and site For best results a rich moisture-retentive neutral to acid soil is required. Alkaline soil will be tolerated just so long as it is deep and fertile. Lots of hot summer sun leads to a fantastic crop of buds in spring but plants require early morning shade once blooming starts to keep frost damage to a minimum. Most people like to show off *M. stellata* in their front garden; if yours is sunny in the morning and shaded in the afternoon you'll earn sympathy not praise.

Year-round care No routine pruning is required but branches are brittle and can snap off in gales or under heavy snow so you might have to tidy things up occasionally. All magnolias appreciate a generous organic mulch in autumn, especially when growing in alkaline soil. Don't use spent mushroom compost – it contains lime.

narcissus

Don't teach your grandmother... If you can read this book without moving your lips you can be safely left alone with your chosen bulbs. Sir Thomas and I merely offer a little fine-tuning. The sooner after purchase you plant the bulbs, the sooner they'll come up in spring. Late summer is perfect. Bulbs planted in late autumn or early in winter will be slow to bloom and short in the stem. Three times as deep as the bulbs are round is my usual mantra. In heavy soil shallower planting is better; on light soil, or in areas prone to penetrating frosts it is wise to plant a little deeper. Deeply planted bulbs are slower to increase by offsets, which can be a good thing when growing bulbs in a lawn as you won't be in any rush to lift and divide them. Lazy, shallow planting is a waste of time. Bulbs rapidly produce lots of tiny offsets that take forever to reach flowering size. Do it properly or not at all.

Leave the leaves alone If the bulbs are to fatten themselves up again after flowering their foliage must be left intact until it withers naturally. If they're in grass, don't mow until summer has definitely left spring behind. In generously-filled borders, surrounding plants cover their shame. Fuss-pots who knot the foliage or tie it back on itself with string should either be strung up themselves or shot.

left: *Narcissus cyclaminius* right: *N.* 'St. Keverne'

They may bee kept out of the earth till about Michaelmas, and then 'tis best replanting them, though any tyme in Autumne may serve the turne.

Sir Thomas Hanmer (1612–1678)

Daffodil Although found all around the Mediterranean, narcissus are mostly indigenous to the Iberian peninsula. Funeral wreaths containing the dainty bunch-flowered *Narcissus tazzeta* have been found in Ancient Egyptian tombs; Homer praised its fragrance in his *Hymn to Demeter*. Ovid's self-obsessed youth metamorphosed into the poet's narcissus, *N. poeticus*, with its white petals and tiny red-rimmed yellow cups. *N. hispanicus* was the great Spanish daffodil noted by John Gerard in 1597 and is a parent of most of the yellow trumpet varieties grown today. By 1620, the first recorded daffodils in the New World were blooming from bulbs carried over by prospective English wives for the Jamestown garrison in Virginia. Thanks to man, countless varieties in all shapes and sizes are now cultivated and naturalized throughout the temperate world.

A quick way to describe any daffodil is to break it down into its constituent parts. The outer parts of a flower are collectively known as the perianth. The trumpet is known as the corona. The fused petals of the surrounding corolla are often termed perianth segments. The ubiquitous trumpet daffodil has a corona as long as or longer than the segments; *N.* 'Trousseau' is a rather smart example with white segments around a soft yellow trumpet. A large-cupped daffodil has a corona more than one third but less than the total length of each segment; *N.* 'Vulcan' has rich yellow segments and fiery orange cups with jagged mouths. A plant with a shorter corona is termed small cupped; *N.* 'Rockall' has white segments around a rich orange corona. Doubles have doubled perianth segments, a fragmented corona, or both; *N.* 'Rip van Winkle' has long greenish-yellow spiky perianth segments forming jaggedy flowerheads; the intriguingly beautiful *N.* 'Irene Copeland' has broad white perianth segments intermixed with shorter, narrow, yellow shards of the corona.

Cyclamineus narcissi have perianth segments pointing in the opposite direction to the corona; with only slightly reflexed petals *N.* 'February Gold' is a sturdy and vigorous form excellent for naturalizing in grass; the wild *N. cyclamineus* has narrow, fully reflexed segments on nodding flowers. Jonquils are usually fragrant and have several smaller flowers to a stem; *N.* 'Suzy' is primrose yellow with tangerine cups. Tazettas can have a dozen or so miniature scented flowers per stem; *N.* 'Silver Chimes' is white, *N.* 'Grand Soleil d'Or' has yellow segments with orange cups.

paeonia suffruticosa

Choose the right site In their mountainous homelands Moutans are subjected to high winds, extreme winter cold then dry soil in summertime; they can live as happily in freezing Scandinavia or wet and icy North America as on the baking Côte d'Azur.

Plant deeply Moutans are difficult to propagate so are grafted on to 'nurse' roots of herbaceous peonies that should wither away over time. A definite ridge on the stem demarcating a change in bark texture clearly identifies the union and is just above the soil on most pot-bought specimens. For the graft to develop roots of its own, it is essential to bury the joint 10–12cm/4–5in below ground level, otherwise the rootstock can send up its own top growth and oust your chosen cultivar. Such deep planting kills most woody perennials so don't make a habit of this.

'During the flaring hours of its glory, it so holds the garden spellbound that no sacrifice is too heavy to make for its presence.'

Reginald Farrer (1880–1920)

Moutan peony Spectacular flowers are usually demanding. Captivating they may be but what gardener, hand on heart, can deny ever having breathed a great sigh of relief when some once-prized beauty threw its final strop and flounced off to plant heaven? Well, here's a turn-up for the books: tree peonies require little maintenance, are incredibly long lived, will grow happily in all types of soil, and few flowering shrubs have a wider climatic range. It's a mystery why Western gardeners who universally adore summer-flowering herbaceous peonies (*Hua Leang*: The King's Ministers) have so overlooked the luscious spring-flowering Moutan (*Hua Wang*: The King of Flowers). Oriental gardeners got their priorities right centuries ago. Placed under the emperor's protection during the Tang dynasty (AD 618–960) and featuring heavily in the visual arts right up to the present day, it remains the Chinese flower symbol for springtime. Besides appearing on much Ming period pottery (AD 1368–1644) the stylized flower depicted on countless export *famille rose* tea-services is in fact the tree peony – talk about not seeing something right under our noses!

At 15–30 cm/6–12 in across, full-blown blooms of *Paeonia suffruticosa* reach dinner-plate proportions and with mature specimens ultimately attaining a height and spread of 2m/6ft 6in their late spring display is quite without parallel. In limy soils they are a sophisticated alternative to rhododendrons and camellias, in acid soils they provide mellow contrast. Flowers can be open and cup-shaped with a simple run of petals round an attractive central boss of yellow stamens or so heavily double with crinkled petals that they sink beneath the deeply-cut foliage at the least touch of rain. Most are highly fragrant and colours range from purest white to darkest plum. *P. suffruticosa* 'Horakumon' (Invitation to Abundant Pleasure) is semi-double with beetroot-purple outer petals and a warm ruby centre, 'Reine Elisabeth' has ruffled double blooms that are shell pink with red flushes while 'Da Ye Hu Die' (Great Winged Butterfly) contrives to bear red, white and red and white flowers all on the same bush. Of the all-time greats the coveted 'Rock's Variety', now regarded as a species in its own right *P. rockii*, is the Moutan of connoisseurs: the powdery crown of golden filaments at the heart of this virgin white semi-double flower glows brilliantly against the innermost petals, whose throats are stained a deep velvety maroon feathering outwards to crimson.

pieris

Pieris A few people are born to stardom; others are destined to be character actors – the rest, I'm afraid, are extras. It's a cruel thing to say, but it's true. Plants are just the same. Unless you're a Cecil B. de Mille of the gardening world, you just can't pad out your scenes with a cast of thousands. As director of your little horticultural drama you have to concentrate on the action in the foreground. Besides your stars though, you still need an ensemble of distinguished players to carry the storyline. Audiences don't always know these actors' names, but when they see them around they know they're in for some quality viewing. Layzgennelmen, Messieursdames, meine Damen und Herren, for best supporting genus in an evergreen role the nominations are: *Bergenia* (p.20), for sterling winter groundcover; *Pieris*, for dramatic spring flower and foliage effect; *Prostanthera* (p.109), for early summer colour and year-round fragrance, and finally, *Ilex* for architectural impact and autumn berries. The winner, for a stunning all-round performance in spring shrubberies, is *Pieris*.

Long drooping sprays of pieris flowerbuds first appear in autumn. They are attractive in their own right and bring colour and interest to the winter garden. According to variety, the protective case, or calyx, around each embryonic bloom is either creamy white or coral pink. The stems they are borne along are suffused with the same colour. In extreme cold the dark green lance-shaped leaves, which hover around the 10cm/4in mark, assume dark copper-bronze tints. So far, so good.

At the beginning of spring the small, waxy, urn-shaped blooms begin to open. They are white or pink and resemble lily-of-the-valley both in shape and fragrance. The large multiple racemes are a glorious sight, forming luscious frothy panicles. Rosettes of young foliage emerge bright red then slowly age to pink and creamy white as they grow, before finally turning green. When spring is well underway shrubs are covered in leaves at all stages of growth. It's as if they're wearing harlequin coats of glossy poinsettias. Oscars all round.

The cast list *Pieris* 'Bert Chandler' is 1.5m/5ft tall and rarely flowers but keeps its spectacular young foliage colours for months. *P.* 'Forest Flame' can form a large upright shrub to 4m/13ft high in woodlands; it has white flowers and excellent leaf colour. *P. japonica* 'Dorothy Wyckoff' has dark purplish-red calyces that contrast well with the white blooms; spring colour isn't brilliant, but mature leaves turn bronze in winter. *P.* 'Flamingo' is similar, but the flowers open deep pink, fade to rose then acquire white stripes; it rarely exceeds 2m/6½ft in gardens. Medium-sized *P. j.* 'Red Mill' has drooping white racemes and bright red wheels of young foliage contrasting very smartly with the bright green background of older leaves.

Don't throw a tantrum Did I forget to mention that all these shrubs require acid soil? Oh dear. Well, you're hooked now so the only turning back I'll allow is for you to check out pages 54 and 55 again. Pieris have just about the same requirements as camellias and small specimens are equally happy in pots.

right: *Pieris* 'Forest Flame'

primula

Hands off! The foliage of these innocuous-looking plants secretes a substance called primin which is a menace to 6 per cent of the human population. It can not only cause severe dermatitis but also sensitize the skin to a wider range of plant irritants and man-made chemicals. Allergens like primin are particularly insidious because our bodies' reactions to them are slow and symptoms can take years to develop. By the time you realize something's wrong, the damage has long been done. *Always* wear gloves when gardening, however awkward they might feel at first, however silly you might think you look. Nowadays I can barely touch a plant without something odd happening – and I've only got myself to blame.

Soil and site Primulas like a cool, moist root run in humus-rich acid to neutral soil. They prefer a little shade but can tolerate full sun just so long as they never dry out. Candelabra primulas really only thrive by streamsides but if you want to push your luck by planting them beside an artificial pool put them on the side most prone to overflowing and keep the pond well watered. *P. vulgaris* and *P. denticulata* don't need boggy soil and are much more versatile as garden plants.

Propagation Lift and divide deciduous primulas in early spring as the shoots start to appear. Evergreens can be divided in spring or autumn.

Pests Slugs, slugs, slugs, slugs, slugs slugs, slugs. And slugs again.

left: *Primula bulleyana;* right: *P. vulgaris*

Primrose Comprising some four hundred or so species, the genus *Primula* is widely distributed throughout the northern hemisphere. Constant moisture is a necessity, acid soil is usually preferred. They are to be found along streams in Tibet, between rocks in the Alps, and under hedgerows down English country lanes. They are among the best-loved garden plants in the world and there are countless cultivated forms. The size and colour of the blooms and the manner in which they are held can vary enormously, yet they are instantly recognizable as primulas because the basic flower shape remains a constant. The corolla is all of a piece, usually with five heart-shaped petals (perianth segments, you'll recall) fused at the base to a tube that is often rich in nectar. They have a delicately sweet, honeyed fragrance.

More or less evergreen, the wild primrose, *Primula vulgaris*, which is naturally pale yellow, has been heavily hybridized and can now be purchased in any colour imaginable and in double forms too. Some are exquisite, others, I'm afraid, are over-egged puddings. *P. 'Wanda'*, for example, is positively smothered in simply shaped, rich purple-red blooms with golden yellow eyes; it combines classic good looks with peasant vigour and is so keen to flower it can barely contain itself till the end of winter. Now that's what I want from a primrose. *P. 'Miss Indigo'*, on the other hand, has none-too-generous clusters of ruffled carnation-like deep purple flowers with exquisite white frosting at the petal tips. All very fine in the details, but surely the whole point of primulas is to give a spectacular display from a distance.

For something more striking, choose a different species. The deciduous *P. denticulata*, or drumstick primrose, has densely packed spherical flower clusters topping off 30–60cm/1–2ft stalks. Usually found in shades of mauve, it has a white form *P. d.* var. *alba* and a striking deep-red cultivar *P. d.* 'Glenroy Crimson'. For larger flowerheads, see if you can track down the vigorous and larger-leaved purple *P. d.* var. *cachemiriana*.

Candelabra primroses are probably the most coveted of all. They carry whorls of flowers in tiers up their stalks and take a little longer than other types to get their act together, generally not blooming until late spring or early summer. They are well worth waiting for though and look terrific en masse. You can have any colour under the sun and they mix well too. There's a powdery softness to the blooms, which enables seemingly disparate hues to sit comfortably next to each other. *P.* Harlow Carr hybrids flower from early spring into summer and can reach a height of 75cm/30in. *P. bulleyana* sallies forth into summer the flowers fading from red to orange with age. *P. pulverulenta* has red flowers with purple eyes and can easily reach 1m/3ft; *P. p.* Bartley hybrids are pretty in pink.

Mid creeping moss and ivy's darker green;
How much thy presence beautifies the ground:
How sweet thy modest, unaffected pride
Glows on the sunny bank, and wood's warm side.

John Clare (1793–1864)

pulsatilla vulgaris

Pasque flower · meadow anemone · wind flower

So called because it blooms in Europe around Easter time, the pasque flower's purple sepals produce a green dye when boiled and were once used for colouring Easter eggs. Among the household accounts of Edward I, there is a note recording the use of *Pulsatilla vulgaris*, among other plants, in dyeing and gilding four hundred eggs for a court celebration. Don't try it today. Like many members of the Ranunculaceae family – which includes *Aconitum*, *Clematis* and *Helleborus* – the genus *Pulsatilla* can put Lucrezia Borgia to shame.

Pulsatillas develop fluffy silvery-white seedheads like those of clematis. The stems elongate as the seeds are ripen, the better for their wispy filaments to catch the breeze ready for off. *Pulsatilla* derives from the Latin *pulso*, to strike or set in motion, and the common name of wind flower seems pretty self-explanatory.

Meadow anemone is a descriptive term too. If the wind is to catch the flower's seeds, it needs an open site. Plants thrive on high chalk downs, limestone pastures and calcareous moorland. What gardeners need to be aware of is that *P. vulgaris* not only requires alkaline soil and exposure to the elements, but also likes ground that is dry and free draining. Before you go leaping to conclusions, you might remember that when we looked at *Asplenium scolopendrium* (p.18), I pointed out that a plant that enjoys shade doesn't necessarily like to be damp. Although *P. vulgaris* likes to be dry, it doesn't like to be hot. It is only found in abundance in the wild in northern Europe and Scandinavia and believe me, that means cold. Its long fleshy roots are efficient in seeking out water; its furry stems and feathery foliage keep surface evaporation to a minimum. It is terrifically hardy. Give it a cool airy site and you'll have years of pleasure.

Chalk and cheese You can't simply throw a garden together. Some plants which look like beautiful companions just won't grow side by side. If you thought of putting some pulsatillas next to your primulas when you first saw the photos you've certainly got excellent taste, but you'll have had second thoughts by now. On the positive side, if the last couple of pages disappointed you because your garden is on alkaline soil, you'll be chortling and rubbing your hands with glee. Gardening isn't like flower-arranging: you're dealing with living things. And they don't always get on well with one another. Or with what you've got to offer. But that's life. If a gardener learns anything at all, it's about happy conjunctions.

Propagation The answer, my friend, is blowing in the wind; the answer is blowing in the wind.

ribes

Soil and site Flowering currants are easy-going shrubs. A well-drained soil and a sunny site suit them nicely. A little shade from midday sun keeps yellow-leaved *Ribes sanguineum* 'Brocklebankii' from scorching. Plants in heavy shade flower much less profusely.

Pruning Nancy-boy haircuts do more harm than good. Don't prune at all for the first few years except to train or shape. From then on, when blooming is over, remove up to one in four older, less floriferous stems completely by cutting them out at the base. This achieves three things. It promotes a continuous supply of vigorous young wood, which flowers from its second year on. It leaves a good number of flowered stems behind to fruit in autumn. It keeps plants to whatever size you want them.

Perfect planting Purples, pinky-reds and yellows associate well. Bleeding heart (p.62), daffodils (p.72), honesty (p.69), leopard's bane (p.63) and yellow crown imperials (p.66) all look fantastic in the vicinity of a flowering currant. Use *Rosa banksiae* 'Lutescens' (p.80) as a backdrop and your spring prelude will be finer than many a summer symphony.

Remarkable for the length and crimson splendour of its stamens, a flower not surpassed in beauty by the finest fuchsia.

David Douglas (1798–1834)

Flowering currant From the Arabic *ribas*, sharp-tasting, this genus contains about a hundred and fifty species including the soft fruits *Ribes nigrum* (blackcurrant), *R. rubrum* (redcurrant) and *R. uva-crispa* (gooseberry), each of which has countless varieties. *Ribes sanguineum*, in my opinion a beautiful and sadly under-rated flowering specimen, is the best known of the ornamentals but you might be surprised to learn that this is only one of a whole bunch of gorgeous garden shrubs.

Cheap seedlings of *R. sanguineum* are the butcher's mince of gardens, nasty, pink and insipid. Named varieties are prime fillet, lean, richly coloured and needing little accompaniment. Try *R. s.* 'Pulborough Scarlet' or the more compact *R. s.* 'King Edward VII' for long dangling racemes of luscious red flowers; *R. s.* 'Tydeman's White' for pure white blooms, and slow-growing *R. s.* 'Brocklebankii' for pale pink flowers with Chartreuse-yellow leaves. The matt foliage has a smell both crisp and musky, which gives a tang to the spring air. It provides a harmonious baseline for the high melodic notes in surrounding floral scents. Say

tomcat if you must, I'll continue thinking about civet and French perfume – it all comes down to the same thing. The white-bloomed blue-black fruit is edible but not particularly palatable.

For a different look and smell, try *R. odoratum*, which is also known as the buffalo, golden or Missouri currant. This has yellow flowers with a spicy scent of cloves and cinnamon and bright shiny green leaves that colour spectacularly in autumn, turning sulphur, bright red and maroon before they fall. Native Americans combined the dried fruit with buffalo meat and tallow to make pemmican. The form *R. o.* var. *chrysococcum* has yellow berries that are generally sweeter.

The dangling blood-red single blooms of semi-evergreen *R. speciosum*, the fuchsia-flowered currant, appear a few weeks before the others in mid spring and can be nipped by late frosts. The shrub itself is fully hardy, but to guarantee a spectacular show train its spiny stems flat against a warm, sheltered wall.

above: *Ribes speciosum*

Cultivation All roses like a good rich soil. *Rosa banksiae* is no exception. Nourish the roots and insulate them against cold by applying a thick mulch of compost and well-rotted manure as winter approaches.

Hardwood cuttings Take woody cuttings in autumn that are as thick as a pencil and about one and a half times the length. Firm these into the ground up to their middles in an out of the way place. Transplant them to their final growing site in a year or so's time.

Pruning and training Horizontal wires fastened to the wall make it easy to tie in young shoots. Remove a few spent stems on mature specimens and cut vigorous summer shoots back a little to promote side growth. Do this between late autumn and early spring.

Good companions Banksiae roses provide a year-round cloak of glossy green foliage and require only minimal pruning so are excellent hosts for summer-flowering clematis like *Clematis montana* var. *rubens* 'Mayleen' and *C. m.* var. *Wilsonii*.

left: *Rosa banksiae* 'Lutea'

rosa banksiae

Banksian rose · Lady Banks' rose Out of the hundred and fifty or so species of rose and the many tens of thousands of cultivars, I have no hesitation in recommending this as one of the most magnificent plants of all time.

Oriental in origin, this semi-evergreen thornless climber is unfortunately a little tender. Although it can *survive* extreme cold it refuses to flower unless given hot summer sun to ripen young wood and a warm winter wall to protect its buds from frost. If you think you can find it a suitable home I urge you to give it a try. It can cover a wall of any proportions you care to supply it with, and in late spring and early summer it is smothered with masses of violet-scented flowers each about 2.5cm/1in across.

From time immemorial the Chinese have quietly enjoyed its billowing clouds of bloom as *Mu-hsiang*, wood-smoke, and it is they who were responsible for breeding and perpetuating the exquisite double forms. Westerners have prized them since the early nineteenth century; everyone who sees them in bloom covets a cutting. They are incredibly easy to strike.

The extremely fragrant double white cultivar *Rosa banksiae* var. *banksiae* was sent to Kew Gardens from Canton in 1807 and named for the wife of its director, Sir Joseph Banks. The double canary yellow *R. b.* 'Lutea' arrived courtesy of the Calcutta Botanic Gardens in 1824. *R. b.* 'Lutescens', the single yellow, was first recorded in Peking in 1816 but only reached England via Italy in 1871 as a cutting of a plant grown by Sir Thomas Hanbury at la Mortola which itself was propagated from a specimen in the Botanical Gardens, Florence. The wild single white form *R. b.* var. *normalis* reached Megginch Castle in bonny chilly Scotland as early as 1796 and formed an enormous specimen which *never* flowered until cuttings taken in 1905 finally bloomed in Nice in 1909. Only single-flowered plants bear hips in autumn; the doubles, unfortunately, are sterile.

tulipa acuminata

Horned tulip The tulip was first cultivated as an ornamental flower in Turkey around the beginning of the sixteenth century. In 1554 Augerius de Busbecq was sent as an ambassador from Emperor Ferdinand I to the court of Süleyman the Magnificent. He returned to Vienna with seeds of a plant that ultimately became known as *Tulipa gesneriana* after the botanist Conrad von Gesner who first described and illustrated it in 1561. This is the principal ancestor of most garden tulips today.

European breeders have always favoured cup-shaped tulips with large, rounded petals. There is no denying the individual beauty of these 'improved' cultivars as cut flowers (just look at all those Dutch paintings), but in the garden, dare I say it, they are singularly lacking in grace and dynamism.

The tulip, or *lalé*, of the Ottoman empire was truly exquisite. The Turks favoured slender, etiolated petals coming to needle-sharp points. Western Europeans seeing representations of these blooms in Ottoman art assume they are heavily stylized. They aren't. And they look just as amazing in the gardens of today as they did in Süleyman's courtyards more than five hundred years ago.

Although *T. acuminata* has a species name it is in fact one of the very first cultivars. Early Western botahists, as you might have noticed, often failed to give due credit to the horticultural skills of other cultures and assumed that anything new to them was a wild species and not already a garden variety. The horned tulip, with its dancing, twisting, flame-like blooms looks like a difficult creature to keep yet it is incredibly easy to grow. Just plant the bulbs well then leave them undisturbed to flower for many years to come in the middle of every spring. This is quite a contrast to the usual performance of lifting, storing and replanting necessary to keep over-bred Dutch tulips in good health. There have been some great advances in gardening – you've just got to go a long way back in time to find them.

Check your bulbs Tulips are reared intensively for a mass market and the bulbs can all too easily become damaged or disease-infected during the production process, in storage, or in transit. Only plant bulbs in the peak of health, and if this means throwing some away, then so be it. They should be nice and plump with a dry but firmly intact skin. They should also have a good heft and not sound hollow when tapped with your fingers. They should be free of all signs of mould or bruising and shouldn't smell fusty. Plant them in mid to late autumn.

Soil, site and depth Tulips like a free-draining slightly alkaline soil in a sunny spot sheltered from wind. On heavy soils add grit. On acid soils add a scattering of Dolomitic limestone when back-filling the hole. Tulips like to snuggle in deep. Bury them up to 30cm/12in below ground in a light soil and around 15cm/6in deep in heavy soil.

Turkish delight For a striking contrast grow *T. acuminata* beside fine-leaved, silver-grey *Artemisia* 'Powis Castle' or the lemon-fragrant *A. abrotanum*. Encourage seedlings of the evening primrose, *Oenothera biennis* (p.104), or that old standby the pot marigold, to appear alongside the tulips' fading leaves.

summer

Not only the days but life itself lengthens in summer. I would spread abroad my arms and gather more of it to me, could I do so.

Richard Jefferies (1848–1887) *The Pageant of Summer*

left: *Lilium pardalinum*; above: *Monarda 'Squaw'*

actinidia kolomikta

Actinidia kolomikta The leaves of this deciduous twining climber are really something else. As in 'something else, man' – don't panic, I'm not about to lecture you on discombobulated perianth segments. They are mid-green suffused with purple when young, rough in texture and they grow to about 15cm/6in long. As they mature, the green coloration retreats to the base of each leaf and the tips become creamy white to blushing pink. It's as if the Queen's gardeners in *Alice in Wonderland* have sloshed them in whitewash then slapped on some rouge. They colour best in full sun, but in a warm climate you should site them where they won't get scorched by midday heat. In cooler climes a wall sheltered from chilling winds will help to keep them in pristine nick.

Little clusters of five-petalled blossoms appear in early summer. They smell of lily-of-the-valley and produce 2.5cm/1in long oval yellow fruit in autumn. These are edible, as you'd expect from a close relative of the Chinese gooseberry or kiwi fruit, *Actinidia chinensis*. They are a diverting side-show at the end of a long, hot summer, not the main attraction.

A. kolomikta is fully hardy. It is a native of the Amur region of eastern Siberia, of Korea and Japan – where it is called the cat's medicine. If you see a contented Cheshire-cat grin on your pet's face and an extra spring in his step, chances are he's been clawing and shredding your vine. If you're a sourpuss, protect the lower stems with wire netting. Or try another strategy. Plant up the base for maximum feline satisfaction with a distracting catmint like lavender-blue *Nepeta* x *faassenii*. Or the stunning *N.* 'Six Hills Giant'. While you're about it, pop in the diverting all-heal *Valeriana officinalis* too. Even the most determined moggy in the world will be totally smashed himself, long before he can do all your plants in. Surely the whole point of gardening is to create a pleasure ground for every member of your household and every visitor too?

Off with their heads! The vines are best trained up walls or fences on a series of widely spaced horizontal wires. For maximum leaf cover, young stems should be encouraged to produce as many side shoots as possible. Do this by chopping off the ends of leading shoots in late winter or early in spring. Prune strong laterals back by about two-thirds; trim less vigorous side shoots back to a couple of buds or remove them entirely if they're really weak. To keep established specimens within bounds and constantly rejuvenated, tip out extension growth wherever necessary and remove an old main stem completely every few years to promote the formation of new shoots at the base. Plants have a maximum spread of about 6m/20ft.

Improve on perfection *Actinidia kolomikta* is an ideal host for summer-flowering clematis with the same pruning regime. Clematis 'Nelly Moser' perfectly complements the leaves with its great pink cartwheels; lavender-purple *C.* 'William Kennett' is a gentle contrast. Climbing roses like fragrant blush-pink *Rosa* 'Mme Grégoire Staechelin' and double purple-red *R.* 'Rose-Marie Viaud' work well too. The first madame has especially fine hips.

agapanthus

Cultivation In open ground, plant agapanthus in rich, well-drained soil in full sun. Container specimens need a good loam-based compost. Flowering is most prolific when the roots are somewhat constricted so don't pot them on too often. Protect garden specimens in autumn with a mulch of garden compost and well-rotted manure. Pot-plants need regular dilute feeds from spring until flowering time; seaweed fertilizers are excellent for agapanthus.

Pests Deter slugs and snails by strewing the ground with sharp grit. Water them early in the morning, liberally wetting the foliage and damping down your terrace at the same time. This raises daytime humidity as it evaporates and makes plants less prone to attack from red spider mites and thrips. Never do this in midday sun; water droplets on leaves can focus its rays and cause scorching.

right: *Agapanthus campanulatus*

Africa lily · Lily-of-the-Nile Everyone who sees these beautiful intensely blue lilies falls head over heels in love. They are clump-forming perennials with long strappy dark green leaves that arch attractively. Some are evergreen and decidedly tender. Most species are deciduous – they are hardier but still appreciate protection from bitter winter cold. After all, they've got South African roots. It has long been the custom to grow agapanthus in large terracotta pots on sunny patios and on baking terraces and then move them under cover at the end of the season before the first frosts threaten.

Tubular or trumpet-shaped blooms are borne in multitudes at the top of tall erect stems. These large inflorescences are known as umbels – an easy term to remember because all the flower stalks arise from a common point, as in an umbrella. Some varieties have radiating, pom-pom-like heads where the flowers follow the line of their stalks. Others have pendent umbels where individual blooms hang delicately downwards (the main stem never droops). In-between umbels are described as intermediate. Whether the dingle-dongles dangle or they don't, all African lilies are incredibly graceful and among the showiest plants around. Where many flowers look awkward in pots and require a lot of

ongoing maintenance, agapanthus are little trouble to keep and look their sculptural and monumental best. Tall specimens in decent-sized containers have football-sized umbels at eye-level and the elegant curves of the foliage are all the more accentuated for being well off the ground.

Evergreen *Agapanthus africanus* has deep violet-blue trumpet-shaped flowers in late summer. The rounded umbels range from 15–30 cm/6–12 in across and are carried on 60–100cm/ 24–36in stems. Size comes with age. The well endowed *A.* 'Blue Giant' starts flowering in mid summer, each rounded head of rich blue bell-shaped flowers can rise to 1m/3ft and counting; it dies to the ground in winter, if grown in the ground it should be given a heavy protective mulch. Dark blue *A.* 'Cherry Holley' stands 75cm/30in tall and has intermediate umbels of trumpet-shaped flowers in mid summer; if dead-headed, it will flower again in early autumn. *A. inapertus* has purple-blue pendant umbels 10–15 cm/4–6 in across on ramrod 1–1.5m/3–5ft stems and the leaves are fairly upright too; it flowers in late summer and on into autumn. *A. campanulatus* has loosely rounded umbels of bluebell-like flowers on lovely grey-green stems 60cm–1.2m/2–4ft tall.

alchemilla mollis

Lady's mantle · bear's foot · lion's foot The plant's generic name was Latinized to *Alchemilla* by the sixteenth-century herbalist Hieronymus Bock in his *Kreuter Buch* of 1539. It is derived from the Arabic *al kimiya* or *alkemelych* meaning 'alchemy'. Lady's mantle has long been valued for its magical properties because of the mercurial dewdrops found every morning on its downy pale green leaves. They were a promising ingredient in the preparation of the Philosopher's Stone and gave added mystique and medicinal importance to the plant itself.

According to Nicholas Culpeper it is a potent aphrodisiac and fertility drug, giving 'lust to the work of generacyon'. Not having tried it myself I can't comment on alchemilla's efficacy in that department but I can see how his mind was running. The rounded leaves with scalloped edges certainly do resemble a cloak or mantle. In the Doctrine of Signatures 'lady' flowers suggested the parts or the possibilities of women, and attractive clothes have always been as much for taking off as for putting on. There's a little more substance to his recommendation than that though. Lady's mantle's lovely sprays of greeny-yellow flowers are incredibly fruitful; they set seed so prolifically that you only need to buy one plant to stock your whole garden. Only relatively recently have they been found to be apomictic, that is, they can produce viable seed without waiting to be pollinated. Keen or what? Just how much did Culpeper know?

Widely distributed from the Arctic down to tropical Africa, there are about two hundred and fifty species in the genus, out of which *Alchemilla mollis*, from Turkey and the Caucasus, has become the pre-eminent garden plant. The leaves range in size from great big paw prints that can easily cover the palm of your hand to pretty little handfuls of pocket change. They form lovely rounded hummocks of greenery above which those bountiful airy cymes of tiny Chartreuse-yellow blooms hover all summer long. The flower stems reach a height of 60cm/24in and create a unifying haze between plants of different shapes and colours.

I can never tire of its foliage and flowers. Like good bread and butter, *Alchemilla mollis* is perfect in itself and a necessary accompaniment to grander fare.

Cultivation Lady's mantle grows the biggest leaves and the tallest sprays on rich moist soil in full sun but, to be honest, it does more than well enough *anywhere*. It can grow in dry, root-ridden shade and through tiny cracks between sun-baked paving slabs. It is fully hardy, and in mild and sheltered spots it is semi-evergreen.

Pro creation? Pot-bought plants can usually be divided into a good many smaller specimens to put into the garden. After that, just let them set seed. Paranoid gardeners dead-head the flowers almost as soon as they appear, which is a terrible waste of their beauty. Those with more sense and better taste let nature take its course. Young plants are instantly recognizable and can appear in all sorts of welcome and delightfully unexpected places. Unwanted seedings are easily transplanted or potted up for friends. When enough is enough simply hoe youngsters into the ground or weed them out and compost them.

Year-round care Given its native habitats, *Arundo donax* is surprisingly adaptable to the garden conditions you can offer. It never outgrows its strength unless you feed and water it too heavily when young, then can't keep up with it when fully grown. A tough, moderate-height specimen is far more attractive than a leggy giant keeling over for want of nourishment. If and when the stems die back in winter, leave them until the leaves become too scraggy to bear then chop them to the ground in anticipation of regrowth in spring. (Old stems that survive the winter in cold climates cannot regrow their leaves but can send out side shoots from the leaf axils. They look ugly, but they have their uses.)

Propagation If you've got the strength, clumps can be divided (or hacked at around the edges) in late autumn or early spring. Unusually for a grass, the giant reed can also be propagated by cuttings taken from old stems in spring or by layering in autumn while the canes are still a bit flexible.

arundo donax

Giant reed Mature specimens of this magnificent grass form large stands that can attain a staggering height of 5.5m/18ft in a season. In warm and sheltered regions it remains evergreen; in cooler more exposed sites climates it is only root hardy and dies to the ground each winter, leaving attractive buff-coloured stalks that needn't be cut back until springtime. The rustling leaves can be up to 7cm/3in wide and as long as 60cm/24in. They are closely spaced and carried alternately right up either side of the cane-like stems. Unless you live in the tropics, bamboo pales into insignificance beside it.

Arundo donax grows naturally by riversides and in ditches all around the Mediterranean and was the 'reed shaken by the wind' of the Bible. Archaeological remains show that it has been used for at least five thousand years in the manufacture of wind instruments like Pan pipes. As Spanish cane it still provides the vibrating reed in the mouthpiece of clarinets and oboes and in the pipes of church organs. Walking sticks and fishing rods are also made from the woody stems.

Drier conditions in cooler climates keep plants on the small side (a mere 4m/13ft or so) and, more importantly, keep them from becoming invasive. In good garden soil they only ever form moderate clumps, unlike bamboos which can send up nasty surprises many metres away from home ground. They are best grown either as isolated specimens where their dramatic outline can be fully appreciated but they can also be used in mixed groups of large architectural foliage plants. They can easily throw a small border out of scale, yet are oddly effective in town gardens when grown in containers near the house – that way, they relate to the building, not to your flowerbeds.

Arundo donax itself has rather glaucous sea-green foliage. *A. d.* 'Macrophylla' has broader leaves with a slightly metallic cast but it's hard to tell the difference. *A. d.* var. *versicolor* is a real beauty whose young leaves are broadly margined and striped with white; it is shorter growing and more tender than the species, the bright variegation mellows to cream when the canes reach maximum height in mid summer.

buddleja davidii

Pruning The harder the better. Butterfly bushes put on a phenomenal amount of woody growth between spring and flowering time in summer. New stems easily reach 2m/6½ft and often exceed this. Because flowers only appear on this new wood the shrubs are pruned between late winter and early spring to produce the optimum quantity of new shoots. This means leaving as little of the previous season's wood behind as possible. Now take a deep breath. Basically, you remove all significant stems to within 10cm/4in of their origins, cutting them back to just two or three pairs of buds. For all the old branches you cut away, four to six brand-spanking new ones will spring up in their places. So while you're about it, remove a few really elderly limbs completely to prevent congestion at the base. By the time you're finished, young plants will have been cut almost to the ground and older stumps will be well below knee level.

Out with the old Replace your buddleja with a younger model every three or four years. Hardwood cuttings about 30cm/12in long root easily in autumn. Poke some into the ground near your existing specimen then hoick it out after flowering in a year or two's time. Well-pruned juveniles have the longest panicles and the greatest vigour; length and performance sadly decline with the onset of middle age. Such is life.

left: *Buddleja davidii* 'Nanho Blue'; right: *B. d.* 'Dartmoor'

Butterfly bush · Summer lilac These hardy flowering Chinese shrubs are joys of the mid summer to autumn garden. For colour, for their honey and freesia fragrance, and for luring bees and butterflies with the promise of nectar, they have no garden equal. Yet they are often derided as coarse and common. Why?

Buddleja davidii and its cultivars are easily propagated and they thrive in dry, well-drained soil in full sun. They are fast growing and tolerant of neglect. Unfortunately their easy-going nature invites abuse. Boy, do they get it. Your average garden specimen is an insipid colour, leggy, straggly and short on flowers for want of proper pruning. All too often it is allowed to become a creaking and decrepit old wreck when it should be regularly replaced by vigorous young cuttings. You, you and you, hang your heads in shame!

The species has lilac to purple flowers in dense tapering panicles that can easily reach 30cm/12in – often they're much longer. Although the drabber grey-mauve forms cheer up railway embankments a treat, named varieties have long superseded them for use in gardens. For really deep purple blooms *Buddleja davidii* 'Black Knight' wins the joust. *B. d.* 'Dartmoor' is a rich magenta with panicles to 60cm/24in long. The red-purple plumes of *B. d.* 'Royal Red' are almost as long but rather fatter; it has a less vigorous sport called *B. d.* 'Harlequin' with smaller flowers and leaves with creamy-white margins. *B. d.* 'White Harlequin' has pure white panicles and variegated leaves. *B. d.* 'White Profusion' has white flowers with yellow eyes and plain green leaves which make it more vigorous in growth. Before planting a white buddleja, do bear in mind that the spent flowerheads stick out a mile; in dark-flowered forms these dingy brown plumes don't really catch the eye. To be sure of getting just what you want, I strongly recommend that you either buy your buddleja when it is in flower or take a cutting or two from a friend's plant that you admire. Don't put any faith in the pretty picture on garden centre tags. Even if the plants are correctly labelled, the colour reproduction is hardly state of the art.

I grow buddlejas as much for the crowds of insects that feed on their nectar as for the flowers themselves. For a bumper crop of butterflies season after season, be sure to grow host plants for their caterpillars to feed on. Leave the nettle patch to your neighbours but always have some honesty and perennial wallflowers around. For greater diversity of wildlife I'm sure you can find room for a few if not all of the following: dogwood, hawthorn, holly, honeysuckle, hops and ivy.

All forms of sensory perception are deeply personal and subjective experiences. They depend on our physiological and psychological make-up. I should just mention that there's a very odd thing about buddleja and the human sense of smell. Some people will swear that it has absolutely no scent whatsoever.

Well-chosen and well-grown buddlejas are among the most sophisticated shrubs imaginable. Gardeners who turn up their noses in disdain are simply exposing their arrogance, ignorance and ineptitude.

callistemon citrinus

Crimson bottlebrush · Lemon bottlebrush

Let's play the name game. *Callistemon* derives from the Greek *kallos*, beauty, and *stemon*, a stamen. It is an accurate description. The early to mid summer inflorescences are composed of hundreds of tiny flowers with prominent stamens that are much, much longer than the petals. The pinhead anther at the end of each exuberantly coloured filament is richly dusted in glistening golden pollen. I literally mean gold not yellow: the effect is of molten metal. These beautiful stamens found towards the ends of the woody stems are arranged in spikes (a technical term, believe it or not, for a raceme of more or less stalkless flowers). What other common epithet could this genus go by but bottlebrush?

The flowers of *Callistemon citrinus* are a brilliant red so crimson bottlebrush requires no explanation. But what about the citrus connection? All will be revealed when you snap one of the sharply pointed, tough evergreen leaves in half. They're rich in a zingy oil that smells sharply of lemon zest. It never ceases to amaze me that people can grow the shrub for years without realizing this.

The outstanding cultivar is *C. c.* 'Splendens', which has brilliant scarlet flowers; it is not so tall growing as the species but a little hardier. *C. c.* 'Hannah Ray' has orange-red flowers and a slightly weeping habit; given that callistemons are straggly shrubs already, it's not a great success. If you want your flowers carried closer to the ground opt instead for *C. c.* 'Firebrand', which has flaming cochineal flowers and a compact habit. Unfortunately, I can't recommend the dingy *C.* 'White Anzac'; callistemons take a lot of beating for really vivid reds but if you want good whites then look to other plants entirely.

In their native Australia bottlebrushes reach tree-like proportions. In the average garden small to medium-sized shrubs are the norm. Grow them in the warmest site you've got and plant fellow sun-worshippers at their feet to hide their spindly legs. Plants to consider include the jaggedy sea holly *Eryngium alpinum*, the metallic blue grass *Festuca glauca*, purple-leaved sage *Salvia officinalis* Purpurascens Group and needle-sharp *Yucca filamentosa*. *Prostanthera rotundifolia* (p.109) and a clump of *Verbascum olympicum* (p.112) make good neighbours.

All that glisters is not gold,
Often have you heard that told;
Many a man his life hath sold
But these Sheilas to behold.

Growing conditions *Callistemon citrinus* is a little tender but it is the hardiest of the 25 or so species of bottlebrush. Provided you grow it on a well-drained site in full sun it generally survives all but the coldest and wettest of northern winters. In its native Australia it grows in relatively moist soil so contrary to appearances it likes to be well watered in summer. I'm afraid it's not suited to alkaline soil and it is too lanky to look good in a pot.

Pruning To keep plants as bushy as possible, snip off the flowerheads as they fade to encourage stems to branch. Otherwise, shoots simply continue growing in a straight line beyond the old inflorescence and produce very few sidegrowths.

Propagation You can try rooting semi-ripe cuttings in late summer but the success rate is poor. I'd prefer you didn't squander precious stems trying.

Sugar for my honey The optimum soil for cerinthes is gritty, well-drained and preferably alkaline. Plants colour best in full summer sun and have a profound dislike of winter wet.

Sowing and growing Never leave spontaneity to chance. In idle moments during late summer gather the ripe black nutlets and chuck them wherever you'd like new plants to appear. A lot of seedlings will have germinated by the middle of autumn. As an insurance policy against a winter massacre, hold a handful of seeds back until springtime when all danger of frost has passed. Assess your stock in late spring: consign tired old specimens to the compost heap then transplant autumn seedlings to plug the holes and to fill gaps elsewhere. Pinch out the growing tips of young plants to promote bushiness.

Go for contrast Beware of growing an awful lot of dark plants together, they can be just too overpowering. *Cerinthe major* 'Purpurascens' has a strong, brooding masculine presence whereas *Alchemilla mollis* (p.86), for example, has a diffuse, golden feminine aura. Don't put Alain Delon in a scene where the script calls for Catherine Deneuve.

cerinthe major 'purpurascens'

Honeywort Combining smouldering good looks with an easy-going nonchalance, this charming Mediterranean annual or short-lived perennial is a good mixer and turns heads wherever it goes. The cultivated variety *Cerinthe major* 'Purpurascens' is easily one of the most unusual and covetable plants I know. From the moment of first clapping eyes on it, gardeners know they simply must have it for themselves. And why not?

Honeywort self-seeds freely and is just as easy to grow as honesty (*Lunaria annua*, p.69), except that it is nothing like so hardy. Left entirely to its own devices it can fade away over a few cold winters. To guard against losing your plants simply remember to save an envelope of seed each autumn to scatter around in early spring. This is the sole secret to maintaining a good rolling supply.

C. m. 'Purpurascens' grows to around 50cm/30in tall. The fleshy stalks are clasped by stemless leaves. In form and in colour they resemble florists' sprays of eucalyptus. Not only is the jade foliage enhanced with a glaucous bloom, it is also blotched gun-metal grey when young. Towards the ends of the stalks the leaves gradually metamorphose into smaller more densely packed bracts. When young these are darkly flushed with plum, petrol blue and turquoise. They age to a magnificent grapey purple-black. The bracts protect tubular flowers that are a rich violet-purple outside and creamy-yellow within. These bloom as the stems grow, leaving large, clearly visible black nutlets nestling in their reddish sepals when they fall. The stem tips become increasingly pendulous under their own weight, which helps with the dispersal of seeds. As flowering ends and summer turns to autumn the leaves and stems become richly suffused with purple, so plants enter a rather dashing and debonnaire middle age as their fresh-faced progeny spring up scattered all around them.

To lime, or not to lime? A deep, well drained soil is essential; the rest is fine-tuning. The more fertile the soil, the larger the leaves and the flower sprays will become. Like most members of the cabbage family *Crambe cordifolia* grows best of all on a chalky, alkaline soil. If you garden on acid soil a handful of ground limestone or Dolomitic limestone mixed into the planting hole will be much appreciated. (Never use slaked lime, it's far too harsh and nasty.)

Start as you mean to go on I strongly suggest that you water your crambe only once in its lifetime. Prepare a generous planting hole, firm in your plant and give it a good drenching to allow everything to settle. Then stop. If you hose them like a maniac, young plants won't bother to put out deep enough roots to find their own water, they'll be less stable in the ground and you'll tire yourself out like a tiny little songbird feeding a great fat cuckoo.

crambe cordifolia

Crambe If you were disappointed earlier at not being able to provide the right conditions for the massive-leaved *Lysichiton americanus* (p.70), your time has now come.

This hardy perennial from the Caucasus grows dark green crinkled leaves the size of café tables, which sprout on long stalks from a central crown. The surfaces are bristly and much puckered, the edges jagged and uneven. It's one great big strapping lad, more a good-looking piece of rough than a thug. Plants take a few years to flower, during which time they usually exceed people's expectations of size and shoulder out neighbouring summer perennials. The flower stalks reach 2m/6½ft or so in mid summer with numerous branches carrying panicles of creamy white flowers. To get the full picture imagine a bunch of gypsophila blown up to the size of a small tree. I kid you not. (A warning: the flowers, though sweet, smell more like cat's breath than baby's breath.)

Crambe cordifolia is a very long-lived plant that needs a lot of space. It will eventually smother an area the size of a round dining table so don't put it bang up against a wall or too close to a path. Think carefully before committing yourself to a site,

mature specimens are hard to transplant because they have thick, very deep roots – you wouldn't want to kill one in its prime.

One very successful treatment is to use it as part of a sparse, modern-looking planting of bold architectural plants, perhaps in gravel. Crambe's root system is well-adapted to poor dry soil just so long as it is deep. It looks right and works well with *Elymus arenarius*, that glaucous blue grass often found on dunes, with the sea holly *Eryngium giganteum*, and with *Euphorbia characias* (p.65), *Onopordum nervosum* (p.105) and *Verbascum olympicum* (p.112). Smaller plants to dot around include *Centranthus ruber*, better known as red valerian, *Festuca glauca*, which forms wiry blue grassy hummocks, *Alchemilla mollis* (p.86), *Cerinthe major* 'Purpurascens' (p.91), *Erysimum* 'Bowles' Mauve' (p.64) and *Sedum spectabile* (p.146).

Crambe can work beautifully in traditional borders too, and I hope you're ahead of me by now. Plant around it with spring-flowering bulbs and perennials that go dormant in summer like *Adonis amurensis* (p.16), *Crocus* (p.61), *Cyclamen coum* (p.26), *Dicentra spectabilis* (p.62), *Doronicum orientale* (p.63) and *Narcissus* (p.72).

dierama pulcherrimum

Angel's fishing rod · Wand flower This frost-hardy perennial has beautiful funnel-shaped flowers 3.5–6cm/1½–2½in long and usually pink. They hang from gracefully arching wiry stems that reach an average length of 1.5m/5ft. The flowers are carried at the height of summer in spikes of up to eight blooms, on stalks so slender and thread-like as to be almost invisible. With around eight of these pendulous stalks per stem, the long stems can be weighted almost parallel to the ground. The gently curving grass-like leaves are fresh and attractive-looking all year round, forming clumps about 60cm/24in in height.

Dierama pulcherrimum is easy to grow yet it is rarely planted well. Its overall habit is as important as the charm of its blooms and imaginative siting is required. Bruisers like Crambe cordifolia (opposite) can shade their neighbours into submission. Willowy wand flowers don't have any weight to throw around. You don't hire a supermodel then hide her face in a crowd, now do you?

Perfect plants to grow around angel's fishing rods include Ajuga reptans (p.50), Bergenia purpurascens (p.20), the clump-forming Campanula carpatica var. turbinata 'Jewel' with its upturned purple bell-shaped flowers, the metallic-leaved Lamium maculatum 'Beacon Silver' with shell-pink blooms, and furry Stachys byzantina 'Silver Carpet'. If it ain't low, it's got to go. An ideal site is close to, or beside a pool where the flower-stems can be reflected in the water. Beware of boggy ground though. Too moist a soil leads to problems in winter. Another good position is right at the front of a border overhanging a lawn or a broad path. Although D. pulcherrimum can be tall, it never obscures the view through to plants behind. An interesting thing to note at close quarters is that whereas most flower spikes bloom from the base up, these open from the tips then work backwards.

If you'd like a change from pink try white D. p. var. album or deep purple D. p. 'Blackbird' and D. p. 'Wine Black'.

The gracefulness of this plant, especially for the margins of shrubberies or ornamental water, can scarcely be surpassed. *The Garden* (1874)

Soil and site This South African native likes a rich soil in full sun. The soil should be as moist as you can make it in summer, but as dry as possible in winter to avoid frost damage to the roots. It is a good example of a plant that is better kept well watered during the growing season on a free-draining soil than planted in a soil that is naturally moist all year round.

Propagation Plants are easily lifted and divided before they enter into active growth in spring. Because the long stems sway so much in the breeze, seedlings can pop up in all sorts of unlikely places. In old gardens it is not unusual to find large specimens growing from the tiniest cracks between paving stones. This is quite perfect: the corms are protected from frost in winter, and the soil can't dry out in summer.

No dandelions tell the time,
Although they turn to clocks;
Cat's cradle does not hold the cat,
Nor foxgloves fit the fox.

Christina Rossetti (1830–1894)

Foxglove This poisonous European wildflower has a colourful history and some sinister local names, including dead men's bells and bloody fingers. Whatever their actual origins, the plant's folkloric associations with fairies, witchcraft and druidism served the useful purpose of scaring children away from harm and of discouraging the uninformed from abusing a valuable medicinal herb.

Foxgloves contain high concentrations of cardiac stimulants, which can cause trembling, convulsions and delirium. However, they have such a bitter taste that no one would swallow any part of them if they could help it. If parts of the plant are ingested they induce prolonged nausea, vomiting and diarrhoea so their toxins are rarely absorbed in any quantity. Should your drawing room ever be strewn with agonized corpses it will be because the butler slipped clinically pure digitoxin or digitalin in your guests' Darjeeling, not because cook mistook foxglove leaves for lettuce. So don't deprive the garden.

A biennial or a short-lived perennial, *Digitalis purpurea* grows a basal rosette of coarse hairy grey-green leaves in its first season. Then in its second year, and in any subsequent summers it sends up a 1–2m/3–6½ft tall, somewhat one-sided raceme of tubular flowers 'like unto the fingers of a glove, the ends cut off'. The flowers come in all shades of purple and pink with white-rimmed crimson and maroon speckles inside their jutting lower lips. There is a pure white form *D. p.* f. *albiflora*, which is sometimes spotted and sometimes not. These blotches, which are actually elves' finger-prints, are reputed to guide pollinating honey-bees towards the nectar at the base of the flowers' throats.

D. p. Excelsior Group come in a colour range that includes a soft creamy yellow, but their most exciting attribute is that the flowers go all the way around the stems, giving them a bolder, rocket-like appearance. Another 'improvement' is the hybrid, *D.* x *mertonensis* which at 1m/3ft maximum is shorter than the common foxglove, but comes in an unusual crushed strawberry pink with a coppery tint. In theory, foxgloves prefer dappled shade; in practice, they'll grow anywhere if they like your garden.

digitalis purpurea

Selective breeding A single plant produces between one and two million seeds so a few of these are bound to germinate. Whatever colours you start off with, successive generations revert to the bog-standard pinky-purple if you leave them entirely to their own devices. To hang on to paler flowers for as long as possible, check over seedlings and weed out those plants with dark flushes to their foliage, leaving pale green specimens *in situ*. Or t'other way about if you want rich, deep blooms. *Digitalis purpurea* Excelsior Group quickly revert to the wild type so you have to keep buying fresh seed. *D.* x *mertonensis* comes true to seed if grown alone and can also be propagated by division after flowering, since it produces small new leaf-rosettes at the base.

hosta plantaginea

Paris hosta Hostas are the archetypal hardy-perennial foliage plant. Their shiny, arching, heart-shaped leaves are often plumply pleated or seersucker-puckered. They come in all sizes, colours and proportions. They form stylish and elegant mounds of greenery, yallery and bluery. They lend unparalleled grace to plantings in moist, dappled shade.

But, but, but... slugs, those evil masters of the universe, are sworn to eliminate them from the planet. It is an honourable death to fall in pursuit of a hosta. They scorn our puny earthling pellets. They sneer at our silly little beer traps. They laugh at the sight of our ridiculous orange rinds. They will always outnumber us; it is their supreme destiny to defeat gardeners everywhere. Ah hah hah hah!

Well, stuff that.

Slugs generally win the day because the battle is fought on their home territory. The shock tactic is to move your plants into more hostile, open ground. The problem is that the hot sunny conditions so feared by slugs are also anathema to hostas, whose leaves can be easily scorched. This is where *Hosta plantaginea*, its variants and its hybrids come in. They are a bit of a surprise all round. They grow best of all at the foot of a sunny wall or in a pot on the terrace and if given enough heat at the end of the summer they produce tall stems of long, lily-like, extremely fragrant blooms as if from nowhere. These open, a few at a time, late in the afternoon and their heady tropical fragrance hangs heavy on the evening air.

H. plantaginea carries racemes around 60cm/24in tall of 12cm/5in long blooms. *H. p.* var. *grandiflora* has larger flowers but narrower, less impressive leaves; *H. p.* var. *japonica* is similar but has dark green, chunkier-looking foliage. *H.* 'Aphrodite' has double blooms; those of *H. p.* 'Venus' are more double still. *H.* 'Summer Fragrance' has lavender blooms and large mid-green leaves with creamy margins. *H.* 'Sweet Susan' has purple blooms tipped white and a long flowering season.

Anyone for a sun-loving hosta with large, pure white fragrant flowers perfect for growing in a pot? ...Thought so.

Year round care Grow *Hosta plantaginea* in a rich loamy soil that is moist yet well drained. Give them a good mulch each year both to improve the soil and to reduce surface evaporation. As a precaution against commando attacks, strew the surface with grit. Propagate plants by lifting and dividing them either in autumn as the foliage dies back or early in spring before they resume active growth. Old clumps can have such rock-hard woody crowns that the only way to split them is with a sharp spade. A few generous wedges of pie will regrow without much sign of trauma. Mean little wedding cake slivers are neither use nor ornament.

Good companions *H. plantaginea* perfectly complements the sword-shaped leaves of phormiums and looks fantastic beside agapanthus (p.85). Pot-grown specimens flower especially well in conservatories and easily hold their own next to tender exotic blooms. They absolutely do not need over-wintering indoors.

humulus lupulus 'aureus'

Golden hop Humans are a territorial lot. Coveting thy neighbour's wife pales into insignificance beside parking thy car in front of thy neighbour's house. And heaven forbid thou should cutteth back thy neighbour's hedge. When I am dictator of the world my second commandment will be to replace all garden fences with plantings of mixed ornamental shrubs (the first will be to abolish plastic flowerpots), but until then what are you all going to do? Fences have to be kept in good order but, ugly as they are, they also cry out to be disguised with greenery.

If you grow shrubs and woody climbers against a boundary fence it can be hard to maintain adequately in terms of painting, staining or (very poisonous indeed) creosoting. If you don't plant it up you will be able to extend its lifespan considerably, but it will be something of a blot on the landscape. This is where golden hops come running to the rescue. They are carried on rough twining stems, which grow so quickly once winter is over that you see visible results on a daily basis. These vigorous herbaceous climbers provide a dense and colourful cloak of shapely leaf cover all summer long that slowly deepens to green and then dies to the ground each year as winter approaches, enabling you to carry out any necessary repairs.

The bright yellow, coarsely toothed leaves have three, or sometimes five, well defined lobes and can be up to 15cm/6in in length and almost as much in width. The bines wrap themselves like writhing snakes around anything in reach and need little encouragement to romp along a wall, fence or trellis or to climb up a pergola or archway.

The overlapping bracts in the female flowerheads enlarge as the season goes on to form the decorative pinecone-like 4cm/1½in fruits, which are the hops used for brewing beer. Although these aren't always borne so profusely as in the green-leaved hop-plants of commerce, they are a very attractive bonus. Male and female flowers are carried on distinct plants (dioecious – remember?) so men, I'm afraid, are a bit of a waste of space.

A rich head The best top growth is achieved by growing hops in rich deep soil in full sun. Plants will still romp away in shade but the foliage will be light green, not golden.

A good body To get really dense leaf cover, run a row of widely spaced eyelets along the top of your wall or fence and stagger another row along the bottom. In spring carefully thread a length of string zigzag fashion through the eyelets then let the hops do the rest. Even a drunk could cut the string and remove the dead bines in autumn.

Fancy another? Propagate hops either by layering or by taking cuttings from the base of shoots in early summer. Plant cuttings directly where you want them to grow; detach and transplant layers in mid to late summer. That was quick!

Squish a handful of the semi-ripe seed capsules tightly and they wriggle and scriggle beneath your fingers like captive insects – a curious sensual pleasure quite as addictive as popping plastic bubblewrap.

Himalayan balsam · poor man's orchid It's far easier to keep a relaxed eye on a thriving collection of happy-go-lucky shrubs and flowers than to nanny an intensive-care ward of scrawny collectors' weaklings into some agonized semblance of life. Before horticultural snobs scoff, this isn't a lazy approach to gardening. Oh no. It's about keeping a firm hold on common sense while pushing ever harder for aesthetic perfection. But it does give you more time for sitting in a deck chair.

For ease of cultivation combined with exoticism and grace of form, there's nothing I'd rate more highly than Himalayan balsam which, since its introduction from India in 1839, has taken so well to gardens that it has 'leaped the fence' and become naturalized in many parts of Europe and North America. It varies in colour from deep rose through pastel pink to pure white. Individual blooms somewhat resemble snapdragons or sweetpeas, as the uppermost petal is hooded and the lower ones fuse to form a lip. Each single-stemmed plant will bear a good hundred or so flowers from mid summer into autumn. It intrigues me how on earth they stay attached: they nod as delicately on their stalks as the pollen-laden anthers of florists' lilies jiggle on the tips of their filaments.

The really amazing thing is that this self-seeding hardy annual can reach 2–3m/6½ft–10ft in a season. With translucent cane-like stems from 2.5–4cm/1–1½in in diameter, with tiered whorls of leaves up to 30cm/1ft long and with flowers up to 4cm/1½in across, *Impatiens glandulifera* is a plant to be reckoned with. Nothing else makes such luxuriant infill between establishing perennials in a young garden. The luminous white *I. g.* 'Candida' can brighten the least promising of shady locations. And what other annual reaches back-of-the-border height in such record time? By nature a gregarious plant it looks fantastic in large clumps, but it is also worth growing a few single specimens close to a pathway the better to appreciate its elegance and admire the intricacy of its orchid-like blooms.

impatiens glandulifera

Growing is easy Himalayan balsam cuts its suit according to its cloth and is adaptable to any soil and location. In an open site beside water or in rich moist soil it assumes colossal proportions; in a dry sunny border or a shady dell it'll be somewhat daintier (a mere 1–1.5m/3–5ft).

Trouble shooting There are no problems so far as the plant is concerned but scaredy-cat gardeners can have kittens over seedlings. Fear not. Simply hoe down or weed out any unwanted guests on a sunny day in springtime. Because the stems are so glassy and succulent they give up the ghost at a stroke. Remember: the plant is entirely under your control and only persists because it reseeds itself each year, not because it has lurking underground roots.

What's the story? Soak your seed for a day or two in a saucer of water before sowing. This softens their hard outer shell and makes for speedier germination. Keep subsequent root disturbance to a minimum by planting only one seed per small pot. Use a loam-based rather than a peat-based seed compost; this slows plants down a little at first but enables them to integrate more readily with your garden soil when it's time to go outside. Barely cover the seeds with compost, stand the pots on trays on draught-free window sills and water them from the base to keep the soil from compacting. As plants grow, insert a wooden skewer down the side of each pot for them to climb up. Before planting them outside, acclimatize them to their brave new world by hardening them off for a week or two in a cool but well lit porch, shed or garage.

ipomoea tricolor 'heavenly blue'

Morning glory As you'll be well aware by now, I'm not a great believer in fuss and bother. The 7cm/3in diameter flowers of this delicate vine, though, are so exquisitely beautiful and such an unearthly shade of pure sky blue that it's one of the very few garden plants I'm prepared to raise indoors from seed. I'm also rather mean, and I generally think that money spent is money wasted if plants aren't either hardy perennials or won't keep themselves going from one year to the next by freely setting seed. I like gardens that can be added to and improved upon with each new season, not ones that have to be started again from scratch at the beginning of every spring. I'm not averse to luxury though, and there's something so silky, soft and sensual about *Ipomoea tricolor* 'Heavenly Blue' that every few years I give myself an indulgent little treat.

Morning glories must have warmth. Once you've got your little seedlings going there is absolutely nothing to gain from planting them out until the beginning of summer. If the air is the least bit chilly the heart-shaped leaves develop sickly yellow streaks and the growing tips can frazzle and die. To get them off faster than a speeding train or a bullet from a gun, keep them on tenterhooks undercover for longer than you think wise. Then hold them under starter's orders for a week: only when you're about to burst with suspense should you release them into the great outdoors.

The slender stems twine round anything they touch and can be grown on the flat to scramble through your borders or can be sent up fences, walls and hedges as a decorative flourish. Plants bloom throughout the second half of summer and in a good year they'll carry on flowering into autumn. These luminous fairy-lights look breathtaking grown into golden hops and make glorious carnival bunting for brightening up early-flowering shrubs like *Azara* (p.19), evergreen *Ceanothus* (p.56), *Jasminum nudiflorum* (p.37) and *Magnolia stellata* (p.71). At the first snap of cold they're off into the ether.

lathyrus latifolius

Perennial pea *Lathyrus odoratus*, the sweet pea, is a cottage garden classic with a host of modern cultivars in a wide range of colours and with all sorts of frills. Their fragrance is strong yet subtle and they make excellent cut flowers. To grow them from seed simply follow the instructions for morning glories opposite, but put the young plants outdoors in late spring as they're hardier and they like to get off to an early start. To take a shortcut, buy trays of seedlings from your local nursery each year. But what if you just can't be doing with any of this malarkey?

Lathyrus latifolius, the perennial pea, is a southern European native first recorded in gardens in 1596, giving it a head start over its annual cousin of at least a century. It fell from favour because its fragrance is only fleeting but, given that over-bred modern sweet peas no longer smell as they used to, a revival is long overdue on the counts of good looks and low maintenance.

The perennial pea is long lived and vigorous, with stems to 2m/6½ft or more, sprouting pairs of glaucous blue-green leaves about 10cm/4in long. It supports itself by means of tendrils, which are thread-like modified leaves. These move in the air (of their own accord!) until they come into contact with a solid object, then they coil around it like a spring. Where stems of twining climbers sometimes dangle and need a little encouragement, tendril climbers need the odd slap on the wrist to stop them grabbing everything around. Racemes of half a dozen to a dozen magenta-pink flowers are carried in profusion from mid summer into autumn. *L. l.* 'Rose Queen' is pale pink fading to white in the centre; *L. l.* 'Blushing Bride' is white with pink flushes; *L. l.* 'Albus', one of Gertrude Jekyll's favourite plants, is pure white.

below: *Lathyrus latifolius* 'Albus'

Most beautiful flowers like those of the Pease, the middle part whereof is bright red, tending to red-Purple in graine; the outer leaves somewhat lighter inclining to a blush colour.

John Gerard (1545–1612)

Easy-peasy Both perennials and annuals like a rich, moist, open-textured soil in full sun. Grow them up cane or brushwood pyramids or along fencing and trellis work. Propagate perennials by division in spring.

Choices, choices You might like to try two more perennial peas if you can track them down. The everlasting pea, *Lathyrus grandiflorus* has distinguished pink and red blooms that are more stately and orchid-like but carried less freely on wingless stems. Lord Anson's pea, *L. nervosus*, a maritime plant that dislikes winter wet, has long-stemmed racemes of six or so very sweetly scented mauve-blue flowers. If you want to experiment with annuals, the eighteenth-century *L. odoratus* 'Painted Lady' has small rose and white bicoloured blooms with the original powerful fragrance. *L. o.* 'Matucana', also strongly scented, has deep purple and indigo flowers.

Consider the lilies of the field, how they grow; they toil not, neither do they spin: and yet I say unto you, that even Solomon in all his glory was not arrayed like one of these. **Matthew XXVIII, King James' Bible**

lilium pardalinum

Leopard lily · panther lily When is a door not a door? When it's ajar. We all know what a tulip is. We all know what a daffodil is. The same goes for agapanthus, fritillaries and hyacinths. But what exactly is a lily? The question is often answered with an echoing silence. Well, in the broadest sense, *all* of the above plants are lilies as they are members of the Liliaceae family. *Tulipa*, *Narcissus*, *Agapanthus*, *Fritillaria* and *Hyacinthus* are a mere five out of around three hundred genera and have approximately five thousand species between them and goodness knows how many varieties, cultivars and hybrids. Confusing? Not in the least.

In visual terms we all have a clear intuitive idea of what constitutes a lily. There is just one niggling point to clear up. Are the white starry lilies of weddings and the elegant white callas of funerals – so beloved of Morticia Addams – the same thing? Answer, not on your life! Calla lilies belong to the genus *Zantedeschia* in the Araceae family; they are aroids like *Arum italicum* subsp. *italicum* 'Marmoratum' (p.17) and *Lysichiton americanus* (p.70). Like many beautiful blooms though, they have acquired the name 'lily' as a popular tag. 'Real' lilies like the regal lily, *Lilium regale*, the florists' 'longi', *L. longiflorum*, and the Madonna lily, *L. candidum*, belong only to the genus *Lilium* in the Liliaceae family. Glad that's sorted out.

But which of the hundred or so species to grow? I always feel it's rather a disappointment to grow flowers yourself when you can pick up better specimens as cut blooms from a shop down the road. Commercially reared lilies are nannied under glass and are the most perfect and long-lasting cut flowers imaginable. They give you exquisite scent and colour for little cost and you don't have to worry about viruses or bulb-rot. The flowers to grow yourself are those that are strikingly different, impossible to obtain any other way and, preferably, ones that are tough enough to look after themselves once established. To meet these criteria I suggest *Lilium pardalinum*.

The leopard lily is an exquisite beast. Unlike many lilies which are single-stemmed bulbs and rarely produce offsets, this one quickly forms clumps by means of spreading rhizomes. Its sturdy stems attain a height of 1.5–2.5m/5–8ft and carry as many as ten nodding blooms each. These are of the Turk's cap variety, which means the petals curve so far backwards that their tips meet at the base of the flower, forming a magnificent plump turban. Not only are the arching stamens with their dangling anthers fully exposed, the colourful markings on the recurved petals can be seen in all their glory. They are orange-red with scarlet tips, the orange throats overlaid with maroon spots on a yellow ground. Rrrraaoh!

Cultivation Native to western North America, this vigorous sun-loving plant is found wild in marshland and scrub. Unlike many lilies it relishes moist soil and overwinters well. Because the scaly rhizomes dry out easily, it is wiser to buy potted specimens in active growth rather than dormant bulbs. For a long and healthy life enrich the planting hole with plenty of humus. Avoid manure as its high nitrogen content will encourage soft leggy green growth (which might need staking), at the expense of flowers. To boost nutrient levels for optimum flower production mix in a good handful of bonemeal. If you'd rather not use animal derivatives, equal quantities of rock potash and rock phosphate work just as well. Regular dead-heading prolongs the mid summer flowering season. Only cut the stems back in autumn when they are quite dead and brown – that way the rhizomes will be as fat as possible for next season.

Captive breeding Lift and divide established plants in autumn, replanting the rhizomes in well-prepared ground at their original depth (about 15cm/6in).

Big cats Despite their size and brightness clumps of *Lilium pardalinum* never look gaudy because the orange blooms are tempered by so much lovely green foliage. If you're a daredevil try *L. p.* var. *giganteum*, which rears its head at a good 3m/10ft.

meconopsis betonicifolia

Himalayan blue poppy · Tibetan blue poppy These exquisite early summer blooms always evoke gasps of amazement when displayed at flower shows and people will literally fight to buy a specimen or two for themselves. The following year wild expectations of a shimmering sea of diaphanous blue poppies are sorely dashed when nothing whatsoever comes up, not even a bit of greenery. Where did they go wrong?

Do you want the good news or the bad news? The good news is that you might be just the right person with just the right garden to grow Himalayan poppies perfectly. The bad news is that when you buy plants in full glory they are often on the verge of completing their life-cycle. In short, they're ready to die. And nothing you can do will stop them.

At best, blue poppies are short-lived perennials which, when mature, will flower for just a few seasons. At worst they are monocarpic, which means once-fruiting – they flower, they set seed, they're gone.

This knowledge might exonerate you from any guilt you've been harbouring if you've tried them before and failed. The big question is, can it help you succeed with them in the future? The provisional answer is yes.

We've already seen how easy it is to establish a natural rhythm with annuals, biennials and short-lived perennials like Himalayan balsam, cerinthe, honesty and foxgloves. All you have to do with blue poppies is take a rather longer-term view.

Only ever buy small, juvenile plants. If conditions in your garden are right, they will flower in a year or two, or three or four, or five. (I did say you needed a long-term view.) With luck they will set seed. With more luck, they'll flower for a few more seasons before giving up the ghost and during this time they might even produce small offsets in addition to further seedlings. You are now in a sufficient state of enlightenment to attain that sea of blue, subject to prevailing physical conditions in your garden. Nirvana doesn't come easy you know.

It's a hard gardening lesson to learn, but sometimes patience, understanding and, occasionally, resignation are more important than action.

Garden conditions Himalayan blue poppies prefer moist, leafy, open-textured soil that is slightly acid and in partial shade. To a great extent you can control all this by choosing the right site and preparing the ground appropriately with lots of leaf-mould, garden compost and perhaps some grit if your soil is on the clay or heavy side. Good drainage is essential if roots aren't to rot in winter wet. What you can't control, however, is the climate. Cool and damp summers work wonders, hot dry ones don't. Pray, move house or give up.

Year-round care Once you've done the groundwork simply leave your plants in the lap of God. Keep a sharp eye out for seedlings and let them grow *in situ* wherever possible as they resent disturbance. Thriving clumps can be gently divided after flowering.

Many persons prefer the infusion of the leaves to the tea of China.

Henry Phillips (1779–1840)

Bergamot · Bee balm · Oswego tea Dense bright scarlet whorls of hooded tubular flowers are carried in knobby tiers on the 1m/3ft stems of this beautiful and aromatic New World herb. The nectar-rich blooms are magnets for bees and butterflies, and will also attract humming birds if you have them. Bergamot was first noted by the botanist John Bartram in 1743 in the vicinity of Fort Oswego on Lake Ontario. Back-woods settlers were already using the plant as a tea substitute, having taken their lead from Native Americans who drank an infusion of the leaves to treat headaches and sore throats, inhaled the vapours to relieve bronchial congestion and applied the crushed leaves externally to soothe troubled skin. It is anaesthetic, antiseptic and decongestant.

The plant acquired its most commonly used name thanks to its remarkable resemblance in smell to the Mediterranean bergamot orange, *Citrus bergamia*. The oil of bergamot so essential to the production of those two great refreshers eau-de-cologne and Earl Grey tea comes from the rind of the fruit, not the leaves of our friend. This characteristic scent is strongest in the type, the brilliant undiluted red-flowered *Monarda didyma*, but also pervades the hot summer air around its many delicately coloured cultivars, which are mostly hybrids with the larger, but less fragrant, pale mauve *M. fistulosa*.

M. 'Cambridge Scarlet' is one of the oldest cultivars and probably the most widely grown, being exceptionally tall and vigorous. *M.* 'Adam' has cherry-coloured flowers and a good bushy habit. *M.* 'Prärieglut' is a warm salmon red. *M.* 'Prärienacht' is a bright lilac-pink. *M.* 'Croftway Pink' is a soft rose-pink. *M.* 'Beauty of Cobham' has pale pink flowers above prominent purplish bracts and is quite breathtaking. A good white form is *M.* 'Schneewittchen'.

Regular dead-heading prolongs blooming from mid summer well into autumn so choose your colours with an eye to both seasons. The accommodating bergamot gives an awful lot of pleasure for a very little effort – use it generously.

monarda didyma

Easy and vigorous Bergamot, with its lippy flowers, square stems and aromatic leaves, is related to mint. The spreading roots quickly form generous clumps. Keep these hardy plants in top form by dividing them every few years while still dormant in early spring, consigning the tired-out central portion to your compost heap. Rich moist soil in full sun gives the best results, but plants adapt well to leaner fare if given a little shade.

A little parched? Purple-flowered forms are more drought-tolerant than the reds. Plants take their drinking habits from the parent they most resemble: upright and abstemious *Monarde fistulosa* is a prairie dweller; lush *M. didyma* frequents streamsides and woodlands. Don't push their tolerance too far though, or they can succumb to powdery mildew.

oenothera biennis

Lean living This biennial American wildflower reached the botanic gardens of Padua in 1619 and is now widely naturalised throughout Europe. It is perfectly hardy, self-seeds freely, and can be left to fend for itself. It positively thrives on poor thin soils in dry and exposed sites. Young plants are easily mistaken for weeds; if you're too tidy in spring there'll be no crop of flowers the following summer.

Perfect planting Large clumps of evening primroses look messy by day but single plants pass unnoticed. For a shimmering *night-time* effect, scatter the tiny black seeds throughout the garden by cutting down dried stems in late autumn and shaking them like *ju-ju* sticks over the soil. Aim for a good few beside a garden bench so you can appreciate them close up with a relaxing glass of wine in your hand after a hard day's work. Keep an eye out for hovering bats: they swoop from time to time on the fluttering moths.

Handfuls of hauntingly beautiful blooms unfurl each day as dusk falls, spend one magical night in the garden, then curl up and die at daybreak.

Evening primrose · tree primrose In a seminar at a wine and food symposium, a friend of mine was rather disquieted when everyone was asked what foodstuff they felt they most resembled. She decided on pink blancmange, then felt rather embarrassed. I see her as a dark and jagged sliver of couverture chocolate myself, but that's by the by. The exercise set me thinking. My floral alter ego has to be the evening primrose. It is tall, pale and lanky and does its best work by night. But while I'm indoors writing, it's out on the tiles.

By day, this weedy-looking, 1m/3ft plant has nary a bloom in sight. It only ever seems to carry buds and faded flowers. Most odd. Only when the sun goes down does it spring into action. The plumpest of its narrow pointed buds unfurl into bowl-shaped 5cm/2in flowers. Before your eyes! It's like watching time-lapse photography on a nature programme – quite spell-binding and uncanny. The tissue-thin blooms have four large rounded petals

apiece and are a luminous canary yellow. As flowers around them slowly fade from your sight, these have a moonlike glow, so well do they catch and reflect the fading light. They have a warm, dry lemon fragrance sexily spiced with a masculine twist of freshly ground pepper. Where bergamot has a juicy, zesty, refreshing zing and would have us all whizzing round the garden like busy bees, the evening primrose charges the air with eroticism and beckons hypnotically with come-to-bed eyes. That it seduces us is coincidental; its aim is to drive pollinating moths to distraction. After a night of debauchery, the crumpled petals hang limp on their stems and the next few buds swell in quivering anticipation. The performance begins shyly in mid summer, peaks in the long evenings of late summer with a dozen or so well-spaced blooms a night, then slowly fades away in the first half of autumn. Though plants are less prolific in later life, the flowers have greater staying power and don't fade till mid day.

onopordum

Scotch thistle · cotton thistle Reputedly brought back from the Holy Land by the Crusaders, the Scotch thistle was adopted as the clan badge of the Stuarts and became the national emblem of Scotland under James V. Which of *Onopordum acanthium* or *O. nervosum* is the genuine article and which the pretender is a moot point; they are remarkably similar and equally garden-worthy. Both these imposing hardy biennials reach 3m/10ft in their second year. Both are covered in cobwebby grey-white felt. Both have striking silver-grey leaves to 50cm/20in long that are jagged-edged and dangerously spiny. Both have chalky-white stems that branch repeatedly and are always held erect – even the very smallest ones are ribbed with ferocious spiky wings as sharp as bread-knives. The golf-ball to hockey-putt-sized base of each thistle-like flowerhead is a scurfy mace-like globe of sharply pointed bracts. The purple-pink flower tufts are not in fact the petals of a single bloom but hundred upon hundred of individual tubular florets densely packed together. These are 'in *yer* face' plants of the highest order with a real aura of power and vitality and a dominating garden presence. *O. nervosum* is the hairier of the two, with brighter inflorescences. Less vulnerable to winter wet because cleaner shaven, *O. acanthium* is the hardier species and its blooms, though paler, are larger. Toss a coin to take your pick. Chaos reigns anyway as each is often sold as the other. Hey, who cares? We're gardeners, not botanists.

You have to wait an awfully long time for a perennial or a shrub to cover a square metre of earth, let alone soar to the dizzying height of Scotch thistles, so these are incredibly useful plants to grow when establishing a garden from scratch: they fill a lot of space in a short space of time. You will find it harder and harder to make room for their seedlings as your garden matures. Enjoy them while you can and give away as many young plants as possible so that you don't feel guilty when the time comes to say goodbye.

Onopordums have long tap roots to seek out water and to anchor them firmly in place. Well-balanced plants need deep, well drained soil. Alkaline conditions are preferred, but not essential. Sun is a must. Fertile ground produces spectacular results, but giant plants can be dangerously top-heavy or prone to wind damage.

right: *Onopordum acanthium*

Mutual support Avoid having to stake plants by growing them in threes, spaced 50cm/20in apart. The side branches interlock to form a really rigid structure.

Problems and antidotes Transplanted seedlings rarely do as well as plants left in situ because their tap roots are easily damaged. Slugs can make the leaves more jagged than nature intended but the damage rarely shows; I only hope they get the tummy-rumbles. Beware of growing Scotch thistles where passers-by can hurt themselves, and always wear gloves, a good thick jacket and safety glasses (I kid you not) when cutting them down in autumn. The flip-side of this nannying, as the canny reader will discern, is that strategically placed specimens are excellent at discouraging trespassers. Ah hah hah hah!

papaver orientale

Growing is easy *Papaver orientale* stands anywhere between 45–90cm/1½–3ft tall, modern cultivars have stiffer stems reaching to 1.2m/4ft and they are generally less prone to wind damage than the species. Plant in really full sun in good deep soil. The thick fleshy roots dislike disturbance so transplants can be slow to establish, flowering little – if at all – until their second year in the garden. Autumn planted specimens are more likely to bloom in their first summer than those put out in spring.

Routine care Follow a regime of tough love. Fertilize sparingly, if at all, since spoon-fed poppies become lush green aphid magnets.

If plants flag they're probably in too damp or shady a spot – move them somewhere drier and brighter!

Propagation Named varieties are unlikely to come true from seed so increase your stock by taking root cuttings in autumn once all leaves have vanished from sight. With a little care it is possible to do this without digging up the parent plant. Scrape the soil away from the outermost roots with a hand-fork, then cut off a few juicy pencil-thick ones. Plant 8–10cm/3–4in lengths vertically, covering their tops with a good 2.5cm/1in of soil. A cloche is useful for frost protection over their first winter.

left: *Papaver orientale* 'Turkish Delight'; right: *Papaver orientale* 'Cedric Morris'

Oriental poppies Some flowers take a while to catch on, others come and go as fashion dictates, but flaming scarlet *Papaver orientale* with its thistle-like deeply cut leaves and immense yet paper-thin blooms endeared itself to gardeners immediately and is an enduring favourite to this day. Discovered in the mountains of north-east Turkey in 1701, it found favour with Louis XIV before sweeping rapidly across Europe and the New World. Larger (a massive 10–15cm/4–6 in across) and earlier to flower than other poppies, *P. Orientale* is also a perennial – instead of having to reseed each year, you just sit back while the plants get bigger and better. It is notably hardy and tough enough to persist for decades in long-neglected gardens choked with weeds – characteristics that make it an ideal candidate for meadow gardening.

Despite its long garden history it was not until 1905 that the plant's first colour break appeared when Amos Perry found a rose-pink specimen in a bed of seed-grown stock. This was exhibited at the following year's R.H.S. flower show as 'Mrs Perry' and was joined in due course by the acclaimed 'Perry's White' which was graciously taken back by the delighted nurseryman when a customer complained that a plant bought as *P. orientale* had come up as a 'nasty fat white one' instead. Further crossing with *P. orientale* var. *bracteatum* and the similar species *P. pseudoorientale* produced a fabulous assortment of variously formed and coloured hybrids and in the run up to the Great War these elegant and sophisticated flowers were *de rigeur* in all the best borders.

There are now so many excellent cultivars on the market that the gardener is spoilt for choice. My advice is to buy plants you like when you see them in flower – not quite the artless suggestion it sounds: buying blind can prove disappointing as plants aren't always what they're cracked up to be. Labels are notorious for leaping from pot to pot in the night, but more to the point some nurseries sell seed-grown stock of named cultivars when really they should be propagated vegetatively.

Although it is tempting to grow early blooms together for effect this is a mistake in all but the biggest of gardens with the deepest of borders as it leaves you with whopping great gaps later in the year. Oriental poppies are notorious for dying back messily so zealous gardeners cut them back to the ground once flowering is over. In theory this promotes a fresh flush of leaves and gives a few small blooms in late summer; in practice it's a waste of time. The wiser, and quite coincidentally the lazier, option is to let the leaves die back naturally. When in bloom poppies benefit from the support of surrounding plants so just be sure to shove them amongst amply proportioned later flowering perennials whose spreading top-growth will cover their fading neighbours' shame. Maroon or soft pink poppies such as 'Turkish Delight' or 'Cedric Morris' are breathtaking against a silver backdrop. While artemisias are an obvious choice, adventurous gardeners might try the tree purslane *Atriplex halimus* or the mammoth cardoon *Cynara cardunculus*. Stronger toned red and orange poppies work best with shades of green, so no problems finding the perfect complement there.

philadelphus

Green or gold? *Philadelphus coronarius*
'Aureus' is the best all-rounder with beautiful
bright yellow foliage in springtime that
becomes yellow-green with age. When the
blossom has gone, it makes a fine backdrop
for the later blue flowers of perovskia or
caryopteris. *P.* 'Belle Etoile' has large and
seriously fragrant blooms with prominent
yellow stamens and a maroon flush at the
base of each petal. *P.* 'Virginal' is tall-growing
and vigorous with pure white, well-scented
double flowers. Perfect for small gardens,
P. 'Manteau d'Hermine' forms a small,
compact shrub with creamy-white deliciously
scented blooms.

Propagation Hardwood cuttings strike easily
in late autumn. Layering is as simple as
earthing up soil around the base of a shoot.

Pests Keep an eye out for blackfly on young
leaves in spring as they can quickly spread
to other plants. Spray them with organic
insecticidal soap at the first sign of attack:
they are hard to get rid of once established.

Mock orange With its beautiful white cup-shaped flowers
that look and smell like orange-blossom, this easy-going shrub
is one of the best-loved most commonly grown garden
ornamentals. It is a criminal waste that so few plants ever bloom
to their full potential. All they need to get by is any half-decent
well-drained soil and a site in full sun or partial shade. No
problems there, then. The stumbling block is pruning. A good
specimen should positively drip with blossom at the approach of
mid summer and fill the entire garden with fragrance. It should
form an attractive, dense, leafy bush from spring into autumn;
in winter it should be neat and tidy, and not look like a right old
bird's nest. I'm sure yours is in perfect working order, but if you
have an embarrassed friend, here's what they need to know.

Philadelphus blooms on stems grown the previous year. If
you prune in autumn or spring you'll remove most of the wood
that was getting ready to flower and you'll have a pretty poor
show, or a no-show, in summer, (although you'll stimulate a lot of
healthy new leafy growth). If you don't prune at all, for fear of
going wrong, the shrub will get choked up with brittle old wood,
its vigour will wane, flowering will fall away (and the lower parts
of stems will be bare of leaf). Now, I'm sure it didn't strike you as
at all odd when I recommended pruning some winter- and spring-
blooming shrubs immediately after flowering. That's all you do
here, it's just that it seems the wrong time of year. It isn't. Trust
me. Take out a quarter to a third of the stems completely, starting
with the oldest. If you feel the need to tidy up any outer
extremities of the remaining branches, do it with a light yet
decisive touch. As ever, I absolutely forbid any fidgety haircuts.
If a stem tip is clustered with tinder-like little twigs don't ponce
around, cut the lot off. Don't delay, the sooner you do all this
once flowering is over, the better. After three or four years you
(I beg your pardon, your friend) will have a totally rejuvenated
specimen to be really proud of. Well-pruned shrubs average
1.5–2m/5–6½ft in height when mature. To keep them smaller,
remove more stems on a rolling basis. Go to the back of the class
if you so much as thought of cutting all the ends off.

above: *Philadelphus* 'Belle Etoile'

prostanthera rotundifolia

Australian mint bush When this extraordinary shrub bursts into bloom at the very beginning of summer you really need to brace yourself. People will stop and stare, ask you for its name, then beg for a cutting. Looking costs nowt – as they say where I come from. *Prostanthera rotundifolia* trips easily enough off the tongue after a few careful rehearsals, but to avoid blank stares it's actually better to use the common name. Politely decline to hack your garden about for complete and utter strangers. Let the cheapskates buy their own plants – after all, you've just told them what to ask for down the shops. You should even be prepared to write it down so they don't try to pinch a bit. If you think I'm having you on, just grow it and see.

The tiny round leaves are evergreen and strongly aromatic. Rub them gently between your fingers on a cold damp day to release a menthol and eucalyptus vapour with a dark and luscious fruity top-note. On a hot, dry day the sun does all the work for you making the air around each plant smell just like the breath of someone sucking a blackcurrant cough sweet.

The small, lipped, bell-shaped flowers are a bright purple-pink. They are borne in short racemes all over the branches and are barely 1cm/1/2in across. What they lack in size they make up for in numbers. The heliotrope blooms are carried in such profusion that the grey-green leaves are all but hidden from sight. 'Beaut', as I believe they say in the Antipodes.

The unusual colour beautifully tones with any purple you like, *Erysimum* 'Bowles Mauve' (p.64) being a good example. Maddeningly, it clashes with most other flowers. For contrast, plant it next to shrubs with silver foliage, to white flowers and to green-leaved shrubs and perennials that either stop blooming in late spring or don't start until mid summer. If you're feeling timid, *P. rotundifolia* 'Rosea' is a pale pink form and is very pretty indeed but not half so striking.

Well worth the risk The mint bush is nothing like fully hardy but neither is it so tender as many people think. If you can grow rosemary successfully, it shouldn't give you much trouble. If your winters are mild, if your soil is well-drained and if you can give it a warm and sunny site sheltered from icy winds, go on – give it a try. If you're in a colder climate, grow it in a pot and overwinter it in a porch or cool conservatory.

Salon styling At last. You can get out your scissors and comb. This shrub resents hard pruning and only requires the lightest, most superficial trim to tidy it up after flowering. Ask it where it's going for its holidays.

Propagation Semi-ripe cuttings taken with a heel in late summer will root if given winter protection in a cold frame or greenhouse. Don't waste your wood if you haven't got somewhere warm to put it.

romneya coulteri

Tree poppy · Matilija poppy Native to southern California and to Mexico, this tantalising woody-based perennial or subshrub was discovered in 1833 by the Irish botanist Dr Thomas Coulter then subsequently named for his friend and compatriot the astronomer Thomas Romney Robinson. 'Coulteria' and 'Robinsonia' were already taken, so *Romneya coulteri*, the sole species in the genus, cleverly commemorates both men. A luminously beautiful plant with a contrariwise nature, you're damned if you grow it, damned if you don't.

A larger-than-life member of the Papaveraceae, it puts on a fabulous show of sweetly fragrant flowers from the middle of summer until well into autumn. Each bloom is fully 15cm/6in in diameter with a central pincushion-like boss of stamens spilling golden-yellow pollen on the overlapping heart-shaped petals. Good specimens reach a height of 2m/7ft or so and put out lashings of delicately lobed, intensely glaucous sea-green foliage. Slender of stem and hairy of bud, *R.c.* var. *trichocalyx*, formerly considered a separate species, has more finely-cut leaves than the type and carries flowers in greater profusion. *R.c.* 'White Cloud' and *R.c.* 'White Sails' are cultivars with especially large blooms. Tree poppies thrive in poor soil and they are among the most drought-tolerant subjects imaginable – you absolutely never need to water them. Given their sun-drenched origins, they are surprisingly hardy and only require a protective winter mulch in the coldest of climates.

Now for a warning shot across the bows before you go sailing off in raptures to the nearest garden centre. Romneyas are notoriously difficult to get established but eventually, when your funds and patience are equally exhausted, they romp away like billy-o and can be the devil to get rid of. Large clumps are easily kept within bounds by digging up any stems that overstep the mark, but you must also be vigilant for wayward shoots. Thanks to stealthily creeping rhizomes these can pop up unexpectedly in far-flung places and sometimes prove something of an embarrassment. A couple of houses ago I had to go on regular night-time manoeuvres to hoick deserters out of next-door's (thankfully unkempt) lawn and bring them back to base. Such larks.

above: *Romneya coulteri* var. *trichocalyx*

Do not disturb Any light, well-drained soil will do, the sandier the better. To give the fleshy roots every chance of penetrating deeply, fork the earth over thoroughly before planting then leave well alone. For the longest possible flower display choose a hot and sunny spot against a wall.

Prune in spring Cut old and frost-damaged stems to the ground then trim any remaining shoots to a height of around 30cm/12in.

Propagation Suckers usually die of shock if dug up, so transplanting them whole is a waste of time. Short lengths of rhizome sprout easily enough though, as do root cuttings taken in autumn as for Oriental poppies (p.106). Seeds can be made to germinate in terracotta pots if you cover the soil with dried pine needles or rosemary leaves and set light to them. Thar's a fire on the chaparral y'all!

Those blooms are worth the winning – large and frail, built of the thinnest crumpled white silk, almost diaphanous.

Reginald Farrer (1880–1920)

rosa x odorata 'mutabilis'

Rosa chinensis 'Mutabilis' · *Rosa* 'Mutabilis' · *Rosa* 'Tipo Ideale' · *Rosa turkestanica* So how many plants am I talking about here? Just the one, it simply happens to have picked up an awful lot of names in its long garden history. Suffice it to say that there's a rather surreal logic in a chameleon-like rose travelling under so many aliases.

Its slender pointed buds are a vivid orange red. They open a warm honey-yellow with the flame colours of the buds still gently blushing the outsides of the petals. In the centre of each satiny bloom is a lovely loose boss of powdery golden stamens. On the second day, after pollination the flowers change to a soft coppery pink. They then slowly deepen to crimson before the petals fall on the third or fourth day. The colours are at their richest in really hot weather. Bushes bloom continuously throughout the summer, thanks to their Chinese heritage, so you get to see all the different hues shimmering together in the sunshine. They are truly magnificent garden specimens. Although the flowers are short-lived in water, there is something very magical about picking a mixed bunch of roses from a single plant. The sheer simplicity of a tall glass vase of these fragile blooms scattering delicate petals on the table-top beneath is utterly breathtaking.

Each flower is comprised of just five slender petals and measures about 7cm/3in across when fully open. They have a light, airy grace and sprays of flowers are often likened to flights of butterflies. When you see a large bush with its soaring branches in full bloom, you'll realize this isn't at all as fanciful as it sounds.

In really warm climates, or in well-sheltered gardens, 'Mutabilis' can form gracefully arching shrubs with a height and spread of 2m/6½ft or so. The average, though, is just under 1m/3ft. Whatever the setting you will find that plants grow taller trained against a wall than when used as free-standing specimens. Red brick not only sets off the flowers beautifully but also enhances the plum-coloured stems and the bronze tints in the young foliage. Mature leaves are a fresh light green with reddish veins.

Soil and site All roses like a good, moist but well-drained loam enriched with plenty of well-rotted organic matter like leaf-mould, garden compost and horse manure. To keep up the fertility it is far better to feed and condition the soil with a generous annual mulch than to use fast-acting liquid feeds. 'Mutabilis' is so healthy and robust it will tolerate poor soil and partial shade, but it gives its very best on a rich diet in full sun. It does well in containers and produces truly spectacular blooms when grown in a conservatory or greenhouse.

Pruning 'Mutabilis' flowers most prolifically when allowed to build up a decent framework of branches. Late in winter or very early in spring, shorten main stems and strong side shoots by no more than a third, but remove all weak twiggy growth completely. Keep plants within bounds and promote regeneration from the base with the occasional complete removal of one or two tired old stems.

Scrupulous deadheading from late spring onwards prevents hips from forming and so encourages the formation of more and more flowerbuds right into autumn. Age shall not wither her, nor custom stale her infinite variety.

verbascum olympicum

Good in a bed *Verbascum olympicum* flowers all summer long and is the daddy of all self-seeders but a responsible parent. It produces thousands upon thousands of tiny seeds yet never gives you more offspring than you can bear to bring up. The progeny take two or three years to produce flowering spikes of their own. Like *Meconopsis betonicifolia* (p.102), plants are invariably monocarpic, dying out after ensuring the continuation of the species. The young leaf rosettes are incredibly attractive in their own right though, and make excellent weed-suppressing ground-cover so there's never a dull moment waiting for the pay-off. As each plant goes off like a rocket, just make sure there's another to keep you happy next year.

The rhythm method Successful gardening is about establishing natural cycles. The seed keeps well and experiment has shown it can germinate after a hundred years in storage. If you buy a packet, use your noggin and sow it over two or three consecutive years. To get friends off to a flying start, give them several young transplants and a dry spike full of seeds in autumn.

Mullein · Aaron's rod With as many species as there are days of the year, *Verbascum* is a large and widespread genus distributed throughout Europe, all around the Mediterranean including Turkey and North Africa, and into Western and Central Asia. There are numerous hybrids and cultivars, yet all are instantly recognisable as mulleins.

They have tall, phallic flower spikes of silky, five-petalled blooms that are usually pale butter yellow in colour. The leaves are generally hairy, sometimes spectacularly so, and rise up the lower part of the stem in whorls of diminishing size at a gradually sharper angle to the vertical. Their felted surfaces act as sunshades and also minimize water-loss through evaporation. Their cunning arrangement channels any rainwater efficiently downwards to the plants' fibrous roots. To conserve soil moisture and to smother out competition, their large basal rosettes lie perfectly flat on the ground. As if this belt-and-braces approach to combating heat and drought weren't enough to put other sun-lovers in the shade, most verbascums are reliably hardy and thrive on poor, shallow, sandy earth, which most garden plants find intolerable. Literally and metaphorically, they stand head and shoulders above the crowd when choosing specimens for parched and impoverished borders.

Verbascum olympicum is the champion of champions. Its leaves are up to 60cm/2ft long and as white and furry as cotton wool; the plant itself can reach to 2.5m/8ft when fully grown. Unlike its nearest contender, *V. bombyciferum*, which has just one single (though impressive) torch-like inflorescence, the main spike is surrounded candelabra fashion by a mass of simultaneously blooming side shoots.

Visually, this mullein is as stylish and imposing as the Scotch thistle. Viscerally, it evokes a radically different response. Where the onopordums are fierce warriors, *V. olympicum* is a great big, huggable teddy bear. Be sure to grow at least one specimen right up against a path or at the very front of a border where mature sensibilities can admire its fine form, where children can gawp up in honest amazement, and where – with differing degrees of stealth – everyone's fingers can stray towards the irresistibly soft foliage.

verbena bonariensis

Brazilian verbena · purple top You might think that so fashionable a plant as this would be a comparatively recent garden introduction. Not a bit of it. *Verbena bonariensis* has been hovering around for an awfully long time, just waiting for its moment of recognition.

Named for the city of Buenos Aires where it was first discovered, this wiry-stemmed mauve-pink to lilac-purple verbena was grown in England as early as 1726, in what is now the decidedly unfashionable London suburb of Eltham but was then a picturesque Kent village. Using seed obtained from a dried herbarium specimen, Dr James Sherard reared plants that were subsequently illustrated, along with many more of his treasures, in the *Hortus Elthamensis* of 1732 he commissioned from Johann Jakob Dillenius, the first Professor of Botany at Oxford University.

Verbena bonariensis is a tender perennial 1–2m/3ft–6½ft tall, which flowers in its first year and self-seeds copiously. Even if parent plants are lost in a few degrees of winter frost, their multitudinous progeny carry on the family line. It's easy to keep, low on maintenance, and blooms from mid summer into autumn. Just why did it take so long to catch on?

It is spare of frame and lean of limb because its dark green leaves are clustered at ground level in a small basal rosette. The slender, four-sided stalks send out long forking side shoots that are matchstick thin. At their tips they carry button-like cymes to 5cm/2in across of tiny but incredibly vivid five-petalled flowers. The optical effect of so many bright, floating spots of colour is curiously distracting and strangely hypnotic. Try to focus on them and the rest of the garden dissolves into abstraction. Concentrate on the bigger picture instead and a dancing purple haze shimmers behind your eyes. The response is visceral and emotional, not reasoned and intellectual. This was no conventional beauty for the Age of Enlightenment; it's a post-modern masterpiece of Nature destined squarely for twenty-first century acclaim.

The more plants you have, the more dazzling the effect. The more dazzling the effect, the more plants you want.

The shock of the new Like, where's it coming from, man? This South American native loves warmth and sunshine to be sure, but its natural habitats are open sites with *moist to wet soil*. Give plants too dry a spot and they'll be disfigured by powdery mildew. The more fertile the ground, the taller their flower stems. The less fertile, the longer-lived the plants, frost permitting.

A bigger splash As an insurance policy against severe winters and for a prolonged flowering season in good years, save a few seeds for spring sowing when you cut down the dead flower stems in late autumn.

United we stand *Verbena bonariensis* can get top heavy but looks ridiculous staked. Closely planted specimens link their upraised arms and mesh together to defy the wind and rain. Three or four plants look good enough but massed swathes are visually more impressive and can overlay and unify many a disparate planting scheme. The whole is greater than the sum of its parts.

wisteria

A short sharp shock To get the maximum enjoyment from a mature wisteria you need an estate agent not a nurseryman. Buy a house that comes with a well-grown specimen, then learn how to prune it. Assuming this isn't an option, *caveat emptor*. Only buy a plant you have seen in bloom; that way you know it's of flowering age and truly the colour you want. Now you can see why I'm such a fan of buddleja: it gives such a quick return on your investment. If gardening teaches us nothing else, it is that Nature rumbles inexorably onwards, but we are only mortal.

Propagation Life's too short for layering. Get your cheque-book out. The most generous gift to the future is lilac-blue *W. floribunda* 'Multijuga' with spectacular racemes to 1.2m/4ft long.

Pruning Wisteria is like the spring-flowering chaenomeles in that it flowers on short spurs growing laterally from the stems. Once the blooms have faded in mid summer, prune all new shoots back to within six leaves. This discourages wispy extension growth and directs energy towards next year's flower buds instead. In early spring cut these same stems further back still, to within three buds of their main branch. This thwarts any plans the plant might have had to re-grow from the new tip and forces out more flowers in summer than you've ever had before. If you don't adopt this two-tier approach to pruning you'll only ever have a second-rate plant. Put it into practice, and you'll be amazed how it can rejuvenate a poor performer beyond all recognition.

Wisteria Board games bore the pants off me, jigsaws leave me sore-headed, but I never tire of fathoming out connections between plants. Anyone can do it. Compare the flowers up above with those on page 99 and you'll immediately see that wisterias and sweet peas are related. Both are members of the pea family or Leguminosae, which, as you go about your rounds and look at their seed heads, you'll find also includes lupins and clover, laburnum and kidney beans. Some are delicious, some make good fodder plants for livestock, some are dangerously toxic, others are exquisitely fragrant. There are annuals, herbaceous perennials, woody climbers and trees, yet the family resemblance is as plain as the nose on your face.

The two most commonly grown species are the Japanese wisteria, *W. floribunda* and the Chinese wisteria, *W. sinensis*. Superficially they are very similar, but there's a foolproof secret to telling them apart. The former is dextrorse, the latter sinistrorse. Duh? All it means is that the stems of the Japanese species twine spirally up a support in a clockwise direction, while the Chinese species climbs anti-clockwise. The pinnate (fern-like – remember?) leaves slowly start to emerge in late spring and consist of 11–19

lance-shaped leaflets in *W. floribunda*, just 7–13 oval leaflets in *W. sinensis*. The pendent flower racemes appear early in summer: Japanese forms often exceed 30cm/12in in length (think, floral abundance). Both have an entrancing sweet-pea fragrance. They range from white through violet-blue to mauve-purple, but only *W. floribunda* runs to cherry-blossom pink. Both are fully hardy, but in cold areas the leaves and flower buds can be damaged by late frosts so plants benefit from the protection of a warm and sheltered house wall. Wherever you live, full sun is essential.

These majestic plants grow to a ripe old age, developing dragon-like woody stems and limbs strong enough to bend, contort and finally snap iron railings, balconies and drainpipes – though none of us lives quite long enough to catch them in the act. It is a great testament to the esteem in which wisterias are held that such behaviour is tolerated but, climate permitting, it also indicates other, and frankly more beautiful, garden uses. Only when plants are trained over archways or pergolas or patiently raised as weeping trees can their flower trusses dangle truly free and be fully appreciated en masse and in depth as you walk beneath them.

autumn

No spring, nor summer beauty hath such grace

As I have seen in one autumnal face.

John Donne (1572–1631) Elegy IX: *The Autumnal*

left: *Clerodendrum bungei*; above: *Clerodendrum trichotomum var. fargesii*

acer palmatum

Planting your tree Acers prefer a slightly acid to neutral open-textured loam but will tolerate alkaline conditions if introduced to your soil with a great dollop of ericaceous compost mixed into the planting hole. Stake large or grafted specimens to prevent root rock. A good organic mulch helps retain moisture and insulates the shallow fibrous roots against temperature extremes. The ideal planting time is in autumn when the earth is still warm and trees are entering their dormancy. For year-round interest take the opportunity to underplant with winter bulbs.

Pruning and training Formative pruning is best carried out in late autumn. Acers throw out a lot of forking stems so if you want more of a tree than a shrub, establish a strong upright leader from the outset by progressively cutting away weaker side-shoots. This is especially important if cascading varieties are

to be seen to best effect. Winter frost can kill young woody growth that didn't have enough time to harden off over summer, so tidy out any dead wood in spring.

Perfect company Why not select two specimens with different leaf forms and habits, and with contrasting spring and autumn colour to make a fine year-round partnership for any garden? *Acer palmatum* 'Waterfall' has exquisitely cut foliage and cascades as strongly as the name suggests. Bright green in spring and flaming gold in autumn it works well with *A. p.* 'Bloodgood'. Have fun choosing your own combinations.

Short on space? Good dwarf forms for rockeries or containers with colour from spring to autumn include: shrimp to green to crimson *A. p.* 'Coral Pink'; rose to light green to yellow *A. p.* 'Kotohime'; and yellow to green to orange-red *A. p.* 'Mapi-no-machihime'.

left: *Acer palmatum* and *A.p.* f. *atropurpureum*; right: *A.p.* 'Bloodgood'

Japanese maple The leaves of Japanese maples are as finely shaped and as beautifully coloured as flowers, yet they are on show for the whole of the growing season. Then, at the end of summer, they really come into their own, transforming themselves with a brilliant display of fiery autumn colour. The vibrancy of tone depends upon a combination of carotenoid and anthocyanin pigments, the production of which changes from year to year according to weather conditions. The warmer the summer and the cooler the autumn, the more splendid the foliage effect as trees reabsorb their green chlorophyll in preparation for leaf-fall.

Acer palmatum is by far the most protean maple species and gardeners over the centuries have selected attractive seedlings and brought them into general cultivation. From 36 named varieties in 1710 there are now more than 350, and breeders are introducing new ones thick and fast.

A great classic is *A. p.* 'Bloodgood', a large-leaved, strong, rich purple-red form that turns a brilliant crimson in autumn. It also produces clusters of 'sycamore' keys that ripen to brilliant

scarlet. Break them in half and let them spin to the ground for the best helicopters ever. Cultivars like 'Bloodgood' with straightforward palmate leaves have a relatively upright habit and attain a height and spread of about 3m/10ft after ten years and around 5m/16ft at maturity.

As a pick and mix guide to choosing the right plant for the right place, bear in mind the following variables. The more dissected or fern-like the leaves, the shorter, shrubbier and more spreading the tree. Also, finely cut leaves are less able to bear their own weight so will droop gracefully. The more entire the leaves, the more a tree's horizontally spreading branches create elegant tiers of floating foliage. Green-leaved trees are generally the most vigorous and least prone to spring frost damage and summer sun-scorch, followed by purple, red and yellow forms. White or pink variegated cultivars, which look sickly enough when you buy them, are tricky to site and need plenty of TLC. Plants with slender foliage tend to be slow growing, but if you're gardening for the long term do remember that a slow-growing variety isn't the same thing at all as a dwarf one.

Whether you treat them as small trees, shrubs or container plants, their garden-worthiness is beyond compare. Everyone should have a handful of acers up their sleeve.

aconitum carmichaelii

Aconite · monk's hood · wolf's bane Only ever handle this beautiful plant with gloves and, however much you're tempted, never use it as a cut flower. Treat it with all the respect in the world but it's bound to come dangerously close to the kitchen sink on its way into and out of the house. Every part of this hardy herbaceous perennial contains the deadly alkaloid aconitine which is so extremely toxic that sap on a cut finger can cause pain in every limb, induce a sense of suffocation and lead to fainting. Ingestion of even the smallest part of leaf, stem or root can have dire consequences indeed. Numbness of the mouth is one of the first symptoms of poisoning so call for medical assistance while you can. You'll be shocked to learn that digitalis, extracted from foxgloves and itself deadly, is used as an antidote. Gardening books rarely hand out this sort of information and I offer it to underline a very important point: treat everything in nature, yourself included, with the greatest possible respect.

Growing to 1.2–2m/4–6½ft, *Aconitum carmichaelii* is an excellent subject for the middle to back of a border – well away from the reach of children. The rounded dark green leaves are divided into three to five lobes, each with finely cut edges. They are carried around upright hollow stems, which benefit enormously from the support of brushwood poked into the ground as clumps emerge in springtime. Not only is this form of protection against wind-damage more efficient and discreet than conventional staking, it keeps handling to a minimum. Plants are attractive green fillers in summer but reach their apotheosis in early autumn, when dense panicles of large blue to violet hooded flowers begin to open. Their purple tones perfectly complement the autumn-tinted foliage of surrounding plants. Carefully snipping off each plume as it fades prolongs the season with a second flush of blooms from side-stalks lower down.

Pick of the bunch is *A. c.* 'Arendsii' with shorter, sturdier stems than the type and intense azure blue flowers. Plants in the Wilsonii Group are taller growing with looser panicles: 'Barker's Variety' has rich violet blooms; 'Kelmscott' is a deep lavender blue; 'The Grim Reaper', when he comes, is somewhat sombre.

Earth to earth *Aconitum carmichaelii* flowers best in a rich, moist, open-textured soil. It must be given dappled shade to perform well on dryish sites. When plants die down in winter, cover them with a good mulch of garden compost in preparation for the following autumn's display.

Exhumation and reburial In congested clumps where air can't circulate freely, stems become prone to rotting. Don't wait for the problem to arise. Once every three or four years, simply lift and divide the long tuberous roots at the end of the season. Young juicy roots contain the highest concentrations of aconitine: handle them with respect or you'll be personally enriching your very own planting hole a little sooner than anticipated. Ashes to ashes: Dust to Dust.

Among the graves of the natives, which are found round the ramparts of Shanghae, it blooms… when other flowers have gone by, and is a most appropriate ornament to the last resting-places of the dead.

Robert Fortune (1812–1880)

anemone x hybrida

Japanese anemone Autumn is a season for reflection and contemplation, so before reading any further, answer me two simple questions. (a) From the information already at your disposal, where do Japanese anemones come from? (b) Has he finally flipped? The answers are (a) China and (b) Not yet, but I'm close.

The true Japanese anemone, *Anemone hupehensis* var. *japonica* is in fact a native of China (Shanghai, geddit?), originating from a wild form in the province of Hupeh. The first live specimens reached England courtesy of Fortune in 1844. However, it reached Japan as a garden plant at a very early date and was first described in the 1680s by Dr Andreas Cleyer, a German employee of the Dutch East India Company living in Nagasaki. It escaped cultivation and became naturalized throughout Japan, so later botanists simply assumed it to be an indigenous species. It flowers from mid to late summer. The best is yet to come.

A. hupehensis var. *japonica* is not the 'Japanese anemone' familiar to gardeners. It is around 60cm/24in tall, rose-pink and has numerous narrow petals. Shortly after its introduction to the West it was crossed with the tall-growing, white Nepalese *A. vitifolia* to produce what is now known botanically as *A. x hybrida* and commonly referred to as the Japanese anemone.

A. x hybrida has broad, three-lobed vine-like basal leaves, 15–20cm/6–8in long, which are coarsely textured and a handsome dark green. A dozen or more shell pink, saucer-shaped, wide-petalled single or semi-double blooms, 5–7cm/2–3in across, float as light as air on branching wiry stems to 1.5m/5ft tall. Flowering begins late in summer and, with diligent dead-heading, will continue almost to the very end of autumn.

A. x h. 'Honorine Jobert' is a single white cultivar faintly shaded pink on the reverse; it dates back to the 1850s and is still one of the finest. *A. x h.* 'Géante des Blanches' has semi-double white blooms with the flip-sides flushed green. *A. x h.* 'Königin Charlotte' has double pink blooms just a tad smaller, shaded purple on the back.

Growing is easy These versatile anemones have creeping fibrous roots and quickly form large natural-looking colonies that can be divided in early spring. They thrive in moist, humus-rich ground and are partial to chalk, but any good garden soil will do. In wild settings they are often planted alongside lightly shaded woodland paths but they are perfectly happy in full sun just so long as they never dry out in summer. Because of their height they can be grown at the back of a border but because their flower-stalks are so thin and the leaves relatively low-growing, they also work well towards the front.

Perfect planting *Anemone x hybrida* looks beautiful in autumn with *Aconitum carmichaelii* (opposite), *Actaea simplex* and *Hypericum calycinum* (p.136), all differing in height, form or flower colour. For added effect, *Clematis viticella* can be allowed to run over the leaves. Anemone foliage is excellent for hiding the fading leaves of *Adonis vernalis* (p.16) and daffodils in sunny sites, and for *Dicentra spectabilis* (p.62) and *Polygonatum x hybridum* in shade.

aster novae-angliae

Soil and site Any moist but free-draining soil will do. Incorporate as much humus as possible at planting time to prevent the ground drying out towards the end of summer while the flower buds are forming. For clumps really to flower their socks off, they must be given an open position in full sun.

Star treatment Because the tall stems carry so many blooms they can become top-heavy unless propped up with brushwood from an early age. The greenery of well-supported plants makes an excellent host for the heavenly blue trumpets of *Ipomoea tricolor* (p.98) in summertime. If your garden is particularly vulnerable to wind damage, either restrict yourself to low-growing cultivars only, or plant tall-growing specimens in relatively dry and infertile sites deliberately to keep their height in check.

The next generation Asters grow into large clumps at warp speed. Split them every two or three years in springtime and discard the tired old centre portions. Happy plants produce large crops of spring seedlings. Unless you're lucky they won't be half so attractive as their parents so I suggest you hoe them down.

To boldly go Massed plantings of different cultivars look out of this world. We don't all have large gardens though, and just a single clump looks fantastic associated with dahlias, echinacea, eupatorium, sedums, Japanese lanterns and Japanese anemones.

left: *Aster novae-angliae* 'Purple Dome'; right: *A. novae-angliae* 'Andenken an Alma Pötschke'

Michaelmas daisy · New England aster

The Compositae or daisy family is enormous, and accounts for more than a tenth of all the world's flowers. What appear to be single blooms are in fact composed of masses of individual florets united in one head. These florets are of two different kinds. Disk florets are tubular and generally form the center of an inflorescence, whether the hard knobby 'eye' of a daisy or the thistle-like head of an onopordum. Ray florets are strap-shaped and assume the role of petals – the 'petals' of sunflowers and florists' chrysanthemums are in fact ray florets. They are all fixed onto the fleshy tip of the flower stem, which is known as the receptacle. It's what's left behind when you blow away the seeds of a dandelion clock and it's the succulent heart of an artichoke. An aggregation of bracts protects the receptacle and this is called the involucre. From now on you'll see composites wherever you turn.

Aster is beautifully descriptive, being Greek for star. Something ill-starred is a disaster, and too often plants from this genus are a disgrace. It's time to put them back in the firmament. Cast all thoughts of wishy-washy, dingy mauve weaklings from your mind. The hot money is on New England asters. These hardy North American perennials reach heights in excess of 1.5m/5ft. Their flower heads can achieve diameters of 5cm/2in or more and are carried in great bunches to 30cm/12in across. The colours are strong and bright. The hairy narrow leaves are impervious to mildew. Clumps illuminate the garden from late summer till the middle of autumn like giant supernovas. With scrupulous dead heading they can be persuaded to twinkle on to the end of the season before being allowed to fizzle away to a few fluffy grey seedheads rimed with frost.

Aster novae-angliae 'Herbstschnee' has pure white rays and rich golden-yellow disk florets; at 1m/3ft or so, it is relatively low-growing and carries sprays of 60–80 blooms. Good rose pinks include 'Barr's Pink', 'Honeysong Pink', 'Quinton Menzies' and 'Rosa Sieger'. 'Harrington's Pink' is especially commendable since its flowers, though smaller than many, appear late in the season. 'Andenken an Alma Pötschke' hat wunderbare kirschrote (cerise) Blüten mit einer goldenen Mitte. 'Crimson Beauty' speaks for itself and is one of the last to arrive at the ball. The imposing 'Stormcloud' reaches a massive 1.8m/6ft and when it finally breaks it's purple-red. 'Barr's Blue' is purple-blue and of average height. 'Purple Dome' forms low mounds with small, very late violet-purple flower heads. 'Violetta' has loose sprays to 1.5m/5ft that require careful support, but rewards you with beautiful blooms of deepest, darkest purple.

callicarpa bodinieri

Soil and site Plant this hardy woodland shrub in a sheltered location in full sun or partial shade. Any decent loam well enriched with garden compost, leaf mould or manure will do. Some chalk can be tolerated.

Year-round care Young plants only require the odd cosmetic snip in spring to remove dead wood or awkwardly growing stems. Once they've attained your desired height and spread, keep mature specimens within bounds by completely removing just a few old stems annually; this maintains an attractive open habit and promotes basal regrowth and regeneration. Mulch generously after pruning. If stems begin to tear under the weight of their berries, cut all damage away and use the trimmings indoors as a change from cut flowers.

By the end of summer it's easy to think you've seen every colour under the sun. Now rub your eyes in disbelief!

Beauty berry Season of mists and mellow fruitfulness be damned – how about a splash of real colour for the dull days ahead? Weirdly, devastatingly attractive, callicarpas are quite simply the sexiest shrubs I know; their fruits outshine even the brightest of summer flowers. Different species originate from the Americas, the West Indies, India and the Orient. While I wouldn't say no to any of them, the one to make my heart skip a beat is the most densely berried, intensely hued cultivar of a Chinese strain: *Callicarpa bodinieri* var. *giraldii* 'Profusion'. Like a Hollywood legend making a grand entrance or like a rock star performing hours later than scheduled, the beauty berry knows how to tease and to tantalize. Passing incognito for much of the year as a useful but unexceptional green filler, when it finally steps into the spotlight before a hushed and expectant audience, the effect is electric. From early autumn until well into winter its slender arching branches are choked with tiers of tightly packed metallic berries in psychedelic mauve – imagine ball-bearings lacquered pink and Parma violet and you begin to get the picture.

This exotic gem would look equally at home outside a gingerbread house or in an episode of Star Trek, yet it's a pushover to grow – the only difficulty lies in finding a nursery that sells it. Plant middle-height 'Profusion' between dumpy pink hydrangeas and soaring plumes of dark purple buddleja (p.88) for a stunning late summer display where, besides mediating well in habit while its own shining hour approaches, its dainty lilac-pink flower clusters perfectly complement these showier blooms. As the evenings draw in, its leaves first blush purple at the edges then slowly turn a dusky rose before fading to yellow, making a fantastic if temporary foil to the ripening berries that are soon exposed on naked stems in all their glory.

caryopteris

Bluebeard · blue spirea Grown as much for the silver lining of its aromatic leaves as for the aniline blues or purples of its flower cymes, this handsome Asian shrub is hardy in all but the most exposed gardens and a welcome addition to any flower border.

Caryopteris mongolica was found in 1831 by the German botanist Dr. Alexander von Bunge in, you guessed it, Mongolia. It has greyish foliage, light lavender-blue flower sprays and can attain a height and spread of around 1m/3ft. In 1844 Robert Fortune discovered a heavily incense-scented species of similar size growing wild in China, and this subsequently became known as *C. incana*. Its downy lance-shaped, grey-green leaves are coarsely toothed; its flowers are vibrant violet-blue. There is also a white flowering form, *C. i.* 'Candicans'.

We now travel forward in time to England in the 1930s. Nice Mr. Simmonds of West Clandon in Surrey had a lucky break. Chance seedlings turned out to be hybrids of the Mongolian and Chinese species, and *C. x clandonensis* was born. 'Arthur Simmonds' himself is a light airy shrub with rich murex-purple flowers. With dark green, slightly toothed leaves that are silver-grey beneath, he's a charming sight, all a-flutter in a breeze. Arthur now has many impersonators, but only two serious rivals. *C. x c.* 'Heavenly Blue' has lighter green leaves, as downy below but downier above, and these really set off the flowers, which are a truly stunning shade of cobalt. *C. x c.* 'Worcester Gold' has daintily scalloped foliage that is warm yellow-green; the flowers are a piquant purple-blue.

If the colour of caryopteris strikes a chord in your subconscious you won't be too surprised to learn that it's related to *Verbena bonariensis* (p.113), *Callicarpa bodinieri* (opposite) and to the amazing clerodendrums at the start of this chapter (see also p.127). All are members of the eye-catching Verbenaceae family, and they're far more versatile than you might at first imagine. It's tempting and exciting to use them in violent colour clashes or with rich pinks and purples, but when that tires you out they also work well in much gentler schemes. These gently effective garden stalwarts associate beautifully with grey- and silver-leaved plants and bring a hippy-chic twist to pastel beds of soft blues, mauves and pinks.

A light diet Caryopteris needs only moderately fertile soil and grows well on chalk and limestone. It requires full sun but, contrary to popular belief, it is perfectly hardy given adequate winter drainage.

Prune in spring Plants flower from late summer well into autumn on the current season's growth. Resist the housewifely urge to tidy them up after leaf-fall as the mass of twiggy stems helps insulate the crown against frost. Wait until spring when the buds begin to break then cut everything back, leaving short stubs or so of last year's growth. Don't cut into older wood; only rarely will it produce new shoots.

Propagation Take semi-ripe cuttings in late summer or strike softwood cuttings in spring.

below: *C. x clandonensis* 'Worcester Gold'

clematis 'bill mackenzie'

Orange peel clematis I drink an awful lot of coffee. Once upon a time it came in three ways. Black, white, or would you prefer tea? I prefer it black. It now comes as espresso, cappuccino, caffé latte, macchiato, and with all sorts of syrupy nonsense added if you've got the palate of a toddler. You know what black coffee is. I know what black coffee is. So why, nine times out of ten, doesn't the gormless youth behind the coffee-shop counter? To get the equivalent of a simple black filter I sometimes find myself asking for an espresso in a latte-sized cup but topped up with hot water instead of milk. Even then I don't always get what I want. Simple things have got to be right.

Now try to purchase *Clematis* 'Bill MacKenzie' and you'll begin to share my rage. It belongs to the hardy Orientalis Group of clematis, all members of which are in truth quite similar and interbreed freely. 'Bill MacKenzie', though, is far and away the best of the bunch and easily the most sought after. In its comparatively short life it has been variously described as a variety of *C. orientalis* and of *C. tangutica*, and as a hybrid of the two. Fair enough, it keeps the botanists off the streets. However, to keep up with demand, specimens available commercially are often just Orientalis Group seedlings when they should be clones reared by micropropagation or raised from cuttings. If you don't buy your plant in bloom, you may well pick a pig in a poke.

Peaking in mid-autumn, citrus yellow *C.* 'Bill MacKenzie' flowers profusely from late summer to the end of the season. Rounded at the base and pointed at the tip, the four sepals are Chartreuse in bud and as thick and waxy as orange peel. Flowers split open like exotic fruit and hang among the foliage like lanterns. After pollination, their prominent central bosses of pistils turn into gorgeous silken mopheads which decorate the naked stems through winter until blown away by the wind to scatter their seed.

Named for a twentieth-century keeper of the Chelsea Physic Garden in the heart of London, this tonic of a late-flowering climber is just what the doctor ordered.

Easy-peasy lemon squeezy *Clematis* 'Bill MacKenzie' flowers best of all when planted in an open sunny site. Although it is one of the more drought-tolerant clematis it will reward you if you keep it well-mulched. Prune it to within 15cm/6in of the ground at the very end of winter for a strong autumn show. This brutal approach promotes multi-stemmed growth from the base and creates plants which, when mature, will densely cover a wall in a season.

Propagation Friends can share prized specimens by layering them early in summer. Sink a terracotta flower pot full of soil-based compost into the ground and peg a stem into it at a leaf node. First, nick it just below this node to encourage roots to grow and stick a small cane into the pot to attach the shoot to. Keep the whole shebang well watered, then detach the stem and lift the pot the following spring. Presto! A pukka plant! Now, where's my coffee…

clerodendrum

Snug and warm Clerodendrums like fertile, well-drained soil. Give them the hottest, sunniest site you can find and insulate their roots in winter with a thick organic mulch. *Clerodendrum bungei* looks especially fine in a narrow border against a house, where its wandering roots can be contained by the wall on one side and the pathway or paving on the other. If plants survive their first two or three winters you've got them for life.

Pruning Frost-damaged wood should be cut away cleanly in springtime. Besides occasionally removing tired old stems of *C. bungei*, there's little else to do.

Propagation Remove young suckers by a mixture of digging and wiggling and replant them straight away. In a mild climate do this in autumn after leaf-fall. In a cold location wait until spring.

Glory flower · star tree Out of the four hundred or so mainly tropical species in this showy genus, there are two plants hardy enough for garden use and of outstanding merit towards the end of the year. The suckering shrub *Clerodendrum bungei* has large, dark green, heart-shaped leaves covered in fine, purple hairs and grows dramatic clusters of red buds (p.116) that burst into incredibly fragrant pink flower heads. With narrower foliage and a tree-like habit, *C. trichotomum* carries loose cymes of sweet-scented, pretty, white, five-petalled flowers. These fall to reveal unearthly china blue fruit the size of holly berries, embedded for contrast in glistening scarlet stars formed by the persistent fleshy sepals, an unforgettable sight. I'll bet you remember them from page 117.

C. bungei was discovered in North China by Robert Fortune in 1844 and named for botanist and missionary Alexander Bunge. It forms a small thicket of woody shoots from the ground and can reach a height of 2m/6½ft or more. If cut back by frost it re-grows reliably from the base. The leaves can be 20cm/8in or so long and almost as wide across. When bruised or rubbed they have an intriguing pungency reminiscent of the ground-cover plant *Houttuynia cordata*. I find it bracing and oudoorsy. You might beg to differ. To recreate it at home put a wet dog in the back of the car and peel a couple of tangerines in the front seat. From late summer to the middle of autumn, densely packed lipstick-red buds at the tips of the stems burst into bloom, forming great rounded panicles 15cm/6in or so in diameter of tubular, rose-pink flowers with a hint of mauve. There's no disputing their scent: it's a heady mix of lilac, carnations and heliotrope.

C. trichotomum is more resilient in the face of cold and will eventually form a small tree or large upright shrub to a height of around 4.5m/15ft if left unpruned. It will still surprise you with the odd sucker. The leaves are plum-coloured when young and age to green, though the veins, like those of *C. bungei* and *Callicarpa bodinieri* (p.124) remain a tattle-tale Verbenaceae maroon. *C. trichotomum* is usually represented in gardens by *C. t.* var. *fargesii* found in West China in 1898 by the French missionary Père Farges. It is more floriferous than the species so carries more fruit into winter.

Some have also called them Filius ante Patrum, the Sonne before
the Father, because (as they think) it giveth seed before the flower.

John Parkinson (1567–1650)

colchicum

Autumn crocus · meadow saffron · naked ladies

The region of Colchis lies south of the Caucasus and east of the Black Sea. It is where, according to Greek legend, the Argonauts sailed in their quest for the Golden Fleece. Colchicums are reputed to spring from the spilt drops of a youth-restoring potion brewed by Jason's wife Medea.

The medicinal history of colchicums dates back to 1800BC in Egypt, and the dried corms have been used in *minuscule* doses through the ages as a specific remedy for gout and rheumatism. They are still prescribed today, in the form of the drug colchicine, against the same debilitating afflictions of the elderly.

The 45 species in the genus are distributed throughout Europe, all around the Mediterranean, well into north Africa and eastwards into northern India and western China. They grow in sunny, open sites in a wide range of soils and, given sufficient drainage, they are fully hardy and trouble-free. After giving their best, colchicums take a winter breather then send up large tufts of leaves to 30cm/12in long in spring. These die back rather flabbily early in summer, by which time the seeds will have ripened and can be sown immediately to increase your stocks. Alternatively, propagate by dividing established clumps once fully dormant. In the wild, corms are found at great depths, and they should be reburied with an absolute minimum of 10cm/4in of soil above their heads. When planting any precious bulbs in a border, discreetly mark the spot by driving a good length of bamboo cane into the ground, always on the side furthest from your house, leaving just the tip exposed. You can find the bulbs easily enough when you need to just by scraping round between the cane and your house with a handfork like an archaeologist. If you start digging accidentally, the cane alerts you to their presence.

Naked ladies look beautiful in lawns. The longer, end-of season grass helps support their delicate 'stems', which are in fact the perianth tubes – the scapes themselves never see daylight. In beds they look stunning grown through silvery ground covers like *Lamium maculatum*, *Pulmonaria saccharata* (p.43) and *Stachys byzantina*. These not only bolster up the blooms in autumn, they are rumbustious enough to withstand the lolloping foliage when it fades. Purple-flowered colchicums are especially striking in front of the orange-fruited perennials *Arum italicum* subsp. *italicum* 'Marmoratum' (p.17), *Physalis alkekengi* (p.142) and *Iris foetidissima* (p.138) , and below fiery Japanese maples (p.118). Pink varieties positively shimmer en masse and make lustrous tapestries on the sunny side of *Callicarpa bodinieri* (p.124), *Fuchsia magellanica* var. *molinae* (p.135) or *Rosa glauca*. On a more intimate scale, they associate very prettily with plummy-leaved forms of *Ajuga reptans* (p.50), with wiry grey-blue hummocks of *Festuca glauca*, and with the strappy evergreen leaves and violet-mauve flower spikes of *Liriope muscari*.

To die for *Colchicum autumnale* has purple-pink to white flowers in early autumn; *C. a.* 'Atropurpureum' is especially dark; the double form *C.a.* 'Pleniflorum' has lilac-pink blooms; *C. a.* 'Alboplenum' is a double white. *C. speciosum* is larger, with more robust stems; *C. s.* 'Atrorubens' has purple-red petals with white throats; shapely *C. s.* 'Album' is an outstanding pure white form with green-tinted perianth tubes. *C. bivonae* has rosy pink blooms with chequered markings, rather in the manner of *Fritillaria meleagris*; these tesselations are never found in crocuses. White-throated *C.* 'Violet Queen' has large pointed petals with strong criss-cross markings. Multi-petalled *C.* 'Waterlily' has fantastically showy blooms in a rich rose-pink.

Don't do it! Common names can be misleading. Saffron, the warm and bitter spice, consists of the dried, red, three-branched styles gathered from the autumn-flowering lilac- and purple-striped *Crocus sativus*. Crocuses belong to the iris family and all parts are in fact edible. Colchicums, on the other hand, belong to the lily family and are poisonous. To avoid cooking lethal paellas, please note that colchicums have three quite separate unbranched styles that are usually, but not always, white. These styles are surrounded by *six* stamens tipped with pollen-bearing anthers – crocuses have just *three*. Now you can tell the difference, you're very welcome to grow them all together, and I'll happily come round to supper.

left: *Colchicum bivonae*; right: *C. speciosum* 'Album'

129

Humble servants These hardy shrubs are happy anywhere. Given a well-drained soil and the odd light mulch, they'll repay you with years of devoted service. Plants tolerate shade extremely well, but the best leaf colour comes from a place in the sun.

Shiver me timbers Cotoneasters are prone to fireblight. Prevent the disease from spreading by giving sickly stems the chop. Keep an eye out for little moth caterpillars in spring. If you're infested, squish them between your fingers. Big caterpillars are usually butterflies. Leave them alone.

Pruning Snip out the occasional weak, ill-formed or crossing branch as winter draws to a close .

Propagation Take greenwood cuttings in early summer.

left: *Cotoneaster atropurpureus* 'Variegatus'

cotoneaster horizontalis

Fishbone cotoneaster · herringbone cotoneaster

The stems of this versatile deciduous shrub, as the specific name implies, grow more or less horizontally. Their side shoots are so densely ranked on alternate sides that branches at the end of winter resemble kippers at the end of breakfast. The rounded leaves are a mere 1cm/¹⁄₂in long, but what they lack in size they make up for in sheer numbers. They sprout in such abundance as to be almost without intervening spaces. Shiny and dark green, they catch the light in such a way that there's no mistaking the plant's ribbed formation even when its bones are fully fleshed. For this characteristic alone, *Cotoneaster. horizontalis* is a useful architectural feature, and it can be exploited in two quite distinct ways. Free-growing specimens rarely exceed 60cm–1m/2–3ft in height but spread considerably and make beautiful cascades alongside garden steps and are good low-maintenance ground cover for steep banks and large shrubberies. Alternatively, shrubs can be trained vertically up walls. Their dimensions are now reversed, and they can attain a height and spread of 2m/6½ft or so, protruding forward by about 45cm/1½ft. If you have the discipline, all breastwood (outward-growing shoots) can be pruned ruthlessly away during the formative years to create spreadeagled plants resembling hundreds of fossilized ferns. The cream margined form, now known as *C. atropurpureus* 'Variegatus', is especially pretty treated this way.

If the tiny hawthorn-like flowers weren't so besieged for nectar by bees and wasps in the first half of summer you'd hardly know they were there. But, ah! Wait for autumn. Barely a bloom goes unpollinated, and masses of orange-red berries weigh down the green boughs. As the fruits ripen, the leaves gradually turn to flame, in a process beginning along the fishes' spines then spreading to the tips of their fins. They are in no hurry to drop and often remain until the beginning of winter. The skeletonized stems look glorious in snow with their berried treasure, which birds pirate away as hunger gnaws.

dahlia

Dahlia Passions run high with these tender perennials. Some gardeners love them to excess and plant little else. Others loathe them with a vengeance and miss no opportunity for public vilification. The secret of success is to cherish them dearly but to use them in moderation.

Sun-worshipping dahlias are tuberous-rooted members of the Compositae family from mountainous terrain in Mexico and Central America. They come into their own late in summer and remain the very picture of perfection until the first frosts massacre their top growth, and transform them overnight into slithering piles of blackened mush. Frosts are low-lying, so autumn blooms generally last longer on apparently exposed sites than in ostensibly sheltered places that are in fact frost-pockets.

Double-flowered hybrids of *Cocoxochitl* had long been treasured by the Aztecs when the Spanish conquistadors laid waste to their empire in the sixteenth century, but it wasn't until the end of the eighteenth century that plants reached Europe and were named for the Swedish botanist Andreas Dahl. So much for cultural heritage.

Tulipomania is a footnote in garden history compared with the dahlia's inexorable rise. Though there are just 30 naturally occurring species there are now around 20,000 named cultivars, which for ease of description are divided into groups. Depending on the shape and formation of its ray florets, a bloom can be a waterlily or an anemone, a pompom or a ball, a cactus or a semi-cactus, an orchid or a peony. Plants can be great gangling shoulder-height giants or dwarf little mounds you want to pat on the head. Buy whatever most takes your fancy but for maximum value keep an especial eye out for shapely or coloured foliage. *D.* 'Bishop of Llandaff' for example, brings opulent plum-black fern-like foliage to the summer border, which is then crowned with velvety semi-double blood-red flowers in autumn.

right: *Dahlia* 'Geerling's Jubilee'

Year-round care Dahlias feed like pigs at a trough. Even in areas free of deep-penetrating frosts where they can be grown like hardy perennials, their quality deteriorates if you don't lift the tubers every few years and replant them in ground heavily enriched with well-rotted compost and manure. In really cold climates it is essential to dig up the corms annually, store them over winter, then bury them 15cm/6in under in late spring or early in summer. If you're dead keen, rotate your dahlias with modern tulip cultivars whose bulbs can be planted as autumn draws to a close then lifted when their own leaves wither and die. If you can't be fagged, simply apply a thick mulch as winter approaches then cross your fingers. If the worst happens, you can always fill the gap with a few seedlings of *Impatiens glandulifera* (p.97), *Lunaria annua* (p.69) or *Verbascum olympicum* (p.112).

echinacea

Coneflower These good old-fashioned American prairie natives have been doing sterling duty in gardens for centuries. All of a sudden they're the height of fashion, thanks to renewed interest in the healing properties of their thick black roots and to increasing regard for naturalistic planting schemes.

In the classic *Travels in the Interior of America, 1797–1811,* John Bradbury describes how tincture of echinacea was used by Missouri boatmen who had 'experienced unpleasant consequences' from their close contact with the squaws. It has since been clinically proven to increase bodily resistance to infection and is often taken as a general tonic. I can personally vouch for its efficacy in soothing skin when applied externally and in warding off colds when taken internally. The aromatic flavour resembles Angostura bitters; while some of us sip it like a pink gin others force it down like nasty medicine.

Originally lumped together with yellow-flowered rudbeckias, rose-purple coneflowers are now regarded as a distinct genus in the Compositae. The name derives from *echinos,* Greek for hedgehog or sea-urchin. It accurately describes the look and feel of the prominent central boss of disk florets encased in prickly bracts.

Echinacea angustifolia grows no more than 1m/3ft tall and flowers in early summer. When the blooms fade, immediately cut the stems to within 30cm/12in of the ground and a second flush will appear in autumn. While the orange-brown central cone zooms skywards, the pendulous, long, narrow petals hang wistfully behind. It exemplifies shabby chic planting and looks beautiful with *Monarda didyma* (p.103) and hazy feather grass *Stipa tenuissima. E. pallida* is taller but otherwise very similar, and associates well with compatriots like twinkling asters and gleaming goldenrod (*Solidago*).

More conventionally daisy-like and reaching to as much as 1.5m/5ft, *E. purpurea* flowers from mid summer into early autumn. Prolong blooming to the end of the season by the simple expedient of regular deadheading. Knockouts for size *E. p.* 'Magnus' and *E. p.* 'Rubinstern' have horizontal rays; the former's are deep purple, the latter's carmine. The arching ray florets of *E. p.* 'The King' are a dark brooding crimson and make the flowerheads more graceful. *E. p.* 'White Swan', with its pure gleaming shuttlecock rays has shapelier blooms still but, like all of the whites, it is shorter in stature.

The hoedown Plant them any ol' which way you like, pardner.

The lowdown Propagate these hardy perennials by division in spring or take root cuttings as for *Papaver orientale* (p.106). Seed germinates easily enough but cultivars won't necessarily breed true.

Perfect plants Given the support of tall-growing neighbours, coneflowers rarely need staking. If you suffer heavy winds, you'll find that pinching out the growing tips very late in spring gives you shorter, bushier specimens.

Cut and come again Do remember that the regular removal of spent blooms extends the flowering season considerably. You will notice that the central bosses become larger and more prominent with age. If you discard the fading rays of elderly blooms they make intriguing additions to vases and can be used in dried arrangements too. Flowers in their prime are incredibly longlasting in water.

left: *Echinacea purpurea* 'Magnus'

Survival experts All species positively thrive on hard, shallow, dry soils. Chalk and lime are as mother's milk. They are fully hardy, withstand seaside exposure and baking sun, but are just as good in shade. They can brighten areas where little else will grow. Plants require minimal pruning besides the removal of all-green shoots on variegated evergreens.

God bless America E. alatus outshines the Old World E. europaeus. Single specimens grow berries in profusion while the European spindle needs company to perform well.

Perfect planting If you crave the autumn colour of Japanese maples but your soil and site just aren't up to the job, plant E. alatus between E. japonicus 'Aureus' and E. fortunei 'Silver Queen'. In winter the corky stems show up well against their yellow backdrop. For a looser look, Caryopteris x clandonensis 'Worcester Gold' (p.125) is a good partner.

euonymus

Spindle We've all got a demon on our shoulder. Friends' relatives are sometimes so unexpectedly different that, when introduced to them for the first time, we can't help but wonder whether the stork flew a little astray. Whatever we're told, we must wait for the chance sighting of a shared quirk or mannerism, or for the sudden recognition of some hitherto unnoticed physical resemblance – until then, we just can't lay suspicion to rest. It's the same with plants: it seems impossible that some species really belong to the same genus.

If you're familiar with those durable Asian evergreens *Euonymus japonicus* and *E. fortunei*, your patience is about to be sorely tested. *E. japonicus* makes dense freestanding screens of foliage, and its golden variegated form *E. j.* 'Aureus' always appears to be dappled with sunshine. Trailing *E. fortunei* makes good ground cover and with a little encouragement can be used as a climber; *E. f.* 'Emerald 'n' Gold' and *E. f.* 'Silver Queen' are bright and cheerful cultivars. They're useful to have around, but they'll never set the world alight. How unlike their drama queen cousin from the States. Flamboyant *E. alatus* has weird stems,

strange fruit, and long oval leaves that turn scarlet and crimson before falling. This broad, spreading shrub grows about 2m/6½ft tall, and its branches are square in section. With age they develop curious, flat, corky wings that are most exaggerated on rich, moist soils and make great winter curiosities. The late spring flowers are lost among the foliage, but in autumn their coral-pink berries can stop you in your tracks. These capsules split as they ripen to reveal the fleshy orange outer casings – the arils – of the seeds. They dangle lantern-like in showy clusters from the beginning of autumn, while the leaves slowly turn acid green before flaring to brilliant pink and red. *E. a.* 'Compactus' is half the usual height and of a very dense habit, so forms a solid wall of colour and makes a good informal hedging plant.

And just in case you die wondering…I've only once seen berries on the evergreens, after a particularly long and scorching summer. They're damn near identical. But I know you won't believe me till you've seen them for yourself.

above: *Euonymus europaeus* 'Red Cascade'

eupatorium purpureum

Joe Pye weed · purple boneset Indigenous to rich, swampy, low-lying ground from Canada to Florida, this hardy perennial rarely achieves its maximum height in cultivation but nevertheless manages a respectable 2m/6½ft on good soil. It is a fine subject for the back of the border, a mainstay of English cottage gardens and a glorious sight beside expanses of water. The huge domed inflorescences appear from late summer onwards. They are rose-pink to mauve and the colour suffuses the whole of the stem. Their hazy out-of-focus appearance is due to the elongated styles that protrude from the many tubular florets. As the turn-of-the-century American naturalist F. Schuyler Mathews noted: 'A good patch of Joe Pye weed under a hazy August sky produces one of those delicious bits of cool pink, set in dull sage green, such as an impressionist likes to paint.' The finely toothed leaves, which are downy beneath, are carried in whorls. They release a scent like vanilla when crushed or bruised.

Fleet-winged butterflies adore feeding daintily on the nectar, just as great fat clambering bees love to guzzle on echinacea (p.132). Grow Joe Pye with coneflowers in one composition and you can watch the circling insects divide into separate queues for touch-down. What is so clever about the design of all daisies is that just a few swoops from one bloom to another can pollinate hundreds of individual florets.

You might as well search for King Arthur, Robin Hood or the Pied Piper of Hamelin as track down the real Joe Pye. He's a powerful, ambiguous archetype of Frontier medicine: herbalist, snake-oil salesman, shaman and faith-healer. Decoctions of various eupatoriums were used to cure all ills but it is doubtful that the bitter-tasting drinks had any real benefit beyond raising a dramatic sweat. On the dark side, *Eupatorium rugosum* certainly caused widespread sickness and death by tainting the milk of grazing cattle. There is only one preparation I am happy to recommend: take equal quantities of Joe Pye weed, asters and echinacea, mix well in a vase with a little goldenrod and add late-blooming roses to taste. It's the perfect visual anti-depressant.

Patently simple These vigorous sun-lovers do well enough in any soil, but given a choice they would plump for something rich and slightly alkaline. On very dry ground, a little dappled shade helps maintain their equilibrium. Truly spectacular plants require ample moisture throughout the growing season. For a whopper like Thoreau's you really do need marshlike or streamside conditions. However tall they grow, their own cane-like stems are all the scaffolding required.

Propagation By the time plants have died down, the soil is getting cold and winter is drawing on. Lift and divide established clumps the following season just as they're starting into growth again. However tenderly you separate roots when transplanting, some will always get damaged. As a general rule, the later plants go into dormancy and the wetter their soil, the wiser you are to move them in spring.

Brought home a great *Eupatorium purpureum* from Miles's swamp. It is ten and a half feet high and one inch in diameter; said to grow to twelve feet.

Henry David Thoreau (1817–1862)

fuchsia magellanica

Hardy fuchsia Though they pout and posture with all their might, precocious modern bedding fuchsias, bless their little hybrid hearts, are doomed to live fast and die young. They bloom soon after being planted out in early summer, they're worn out by early autumn, then that Grim Reaper frost spirits them away at the end of the season. Youth culture is hard work for gardeners.

Fuchsia magellanica on the other hand, takes a more measured approach to life, and one you will come to appreciate. The origins and the delicate looks of this graceful late-flowering shrub belie a sound constitution. Found wild from Mexico south to Tierra del Fuego this variable species thrives in all but the coldest and wettest of climates and flourishes on windy coastlines. Well-planted specimens reach a ripe old age and in favourable conditions they can attain heights of 2–3m/6½ft–10ft.

Flower droplets pour from the leaf axils in late summer. The effect is exquisite but plants only enter their prime on the cusp with autumn. With the poise of the corps de ballet in Swan Lake stretching their wings, the slender pointed sepals peel upwards horizontally to reveal the central roll of petals around the long, protruding stamens and the even longer style. The blooms are like fairy lights, and there can be hundreds and hundreds of them on a single plant. They last until mid autumn when their juicy aubergine fruits take over the show.

In the type, the sepals and the rest of the calyx are striking scarlet and the petals are a rich violet purple. *F. m.* var. *gracilis* 'Variegata' has green leaves with creamy yellow edges that flush pink with age. *F. m.* 'Versicolor' has grey-green leaves flushed rose when young that become randomly splashed cream and yellow with age. Their bright foliage is attractive in summer and shines behind the blooms in autumn. They do best in light shade. *F. m.* var. *gracilis* is extremely free-flowering and displays its bounty on slender, arching stems. The prima ballerina, though, has got to be *F. m.* var. *molinae*. At first her fragile skirts seem to be white, as the old name *F. m.* 'Alba' would suggest, but on closer inspection the sepals are palest pink, the petals have a hint of lavender and the stamens are rose, not red. Brava!

Plant for life Young fuchsias in pots are small and twiggy so they are rarely treated with the respect they deserve. Prepare a large hole generously enriched with well-rotted compost and a little manure then tap out the plant and position the rootball so the base of the stem is 5cm/2in *below* soil level. This not only provides stability, it protects the roots from frost and promotes multi-branched growth from the base. Take semi-ripe cuttings in late summer for friends who admire your taste.

Pruning and training There will be a lot of dead wood after severe frosts. Cut plants hard back at the end of winter, rather in the manner of buddleja (p.88) and caryopteris (p.125). Use the trimmings of all three to support top-heavy perennials like monk's hood (p.120) and Michaelmas daisies (p.122). Main stems can be wall-trained in mild areas, but fidgety, twiggy growth should still be removed annually.

Rise and shine New shoots and leaves rarely appear until the beginning of summer, so spring-flowering bulbs can be planted right up to the base.

hypericum calycinum

Rose of Sharon · Aaron's beard · St John's wort

With their starburst yellow blooms opening around the longest day of the year, hypericums were potent, pagan charms for warding off evil, long before the early Christian church began grafting holy days on to nature rites. We're all sun-worshippers at heart, so the mid summer solstice never quite caught on as the feast of John the Baptist (You Know Who had an easier job imprinting His identity on the winter one), but the saint's name at least stuck to the plants. They continue bringing 'light to them that sit in darkness' until the middle of autumn.

The largest flowers, measuring up to 10cm/4in across, belong to wiry-stemmed *Hypericum calycinum*. Their golden-yellow petals appear as if blown on their backs by great powder-puff explosions of orange-tipped stamens. The shrub itself stands barely 30cm/1ft tall and sends up numerous shoots from its vigorous creeping rootstock. Although it hails from the eastern Mediterranean, it is fully hardy. The leathery dark green leaves have a resinous smell when crushed, studded as they are with tiny, translucent oil glands. They are retained through winter but some flush yellow and acquire coppery tints before falling. Plants are equally happy in full sun or deep shade, grow well in poor soils, and are incredibly tolerant of drought. Plants introduced to Australia have become a national menace. Few ground covers are so versatile, few border flowers are so beautiful.

The trick to growing perfect specimens, if you've got the nerve, simply involves shearing or strimming them to the ground at the end of winter, then mulching the roots with a thin layer of compost or manure. This seems to go against the grain for what is essentially an evergreen but the result, far from a waste of past endeavour, is a striking rejuvenation. Plants send up more stems from the same piece of ground and they look all the better for their brand spanking new foliage. Most important of all, the flowering season – which now starts later – is longer lasting and more spectacular than you could ever imagine.

Ring the changes *Hypericum calycinum* likes to form large colonies so is excellent for covering parched banks with greenery and for brightening up deep, dry shade under dense evergreens like hollies. If you cut it back religiously each year as suggested then you can build in a little surprise: *Hyacinthoides hispanica*, the notoriously tough Spanish or giant bluebell. Plant its bulbs thickly between divided roots of the St. John's wort and you'll have a spectacular spring flower display too. As summer approaches, you will find that the advancing guard of hypericum foliage nicely covers the bluebell's retreat. Keep your eyes peeled for the elegant, white cultivar, *H. h* 'La Grandesse'.

Quack, quack The benign magical and spiritual associations of St. John's wort have rather fuddled people's attitudes to it as a drug. It is a powerful and dangerous force. Take it under proper medical supervision or not at all. You have been warned.

ilex aquifolium

Common holly · English holly Pay attention, class, and
no tittering at the back. Cast your mind back – or indeed, forward
– to winter, and *Garrya elliptica* (p.32). Specimens carry flowers of
one sex or the other exclusively and males are generally chosen
because their tassels are longer. Hollies are also dioecious, but
because they are grown as much for their yellow, orange or red
berries as for their distinctive glossy and spiky foliage, gardeners
prefer the females. Men do have their uses though, and without
the pollen of their flowers in spring there wouldn't be any fruit
in autumn. Basically, mummy hollies need a daddy holly to get
pregnant. (To avoid embarrassing anyone with a strict
upbringing, should you want lots of plants with berries, please
note the use of plural and singular nouns).

There are more than four hundred species in the genus,
not all of which you would think of putting on your Christmas
pudding, not all of which are evergreen, not all of which are
even hardy – some come from tropical and subtropical regions.
Ilex aquifolium though, conforms to every holly stereotype you
know, can be planted anywhere, and is entirely trouble-free. It
can be topiarized, used for hedging, kept as an informal shrub
or left to grow into a tree as tall as 25m/80ft. Maddeningly, a
cultivar's name is no clue to its gender.

Let's eye up some lads first. The hedgehog holly, *I. a.* 'Ferox'
is easily the prickliest, with spines on the surfaces of its leaves as
well as clustered around the edges; *I. a.* 'Ferox Argentea' has
creamy-white margins and spikes; *I. a.* 'Ferox Aurea' has a central
yellow blotch towards the base of each leaf. All three are sterile.
I. a. 'Golden Milkboy' has a huge bright yellow splash over most
of the leaf, with irregular, bright green and almost black
colouring at the margins. *I. a.* 'Golden Queen' has broad yellow
margins, *I. a.* 'Silver Queen' has white ones. *I. a.* 'Laurifolia' has
smooth-edged darkest green leaves with just a spine or two at
the tip; it flowers profusely and is one of the best pollinators.

Now for the lasses. *I. a.* 'Alaska' grows tall and thin, with
traditional green-black leaves and bright red berries. *I. a.* 'Amber'
has bright green laurel-like leaves and thick clusters of orange-
yellow fruit. *I. a.* 'Argentea Marginata' has white leaf margins
and masses of scarlet berries; *I. a.* 'Argentea Marginata Pendula'
is a weeping form. *I. a.* 'Bacciflava' has olive green leaves with
brilliant yellow fruit. The appropriately named I. a. 'Harpune'
carries just a few red berries but has unusually narrow, spear-like
leaves with the odd vicious spike on otherwise smooth sides.

above: *Ilex aquifolium* 'Aurea Marginata'

Arthur or Martha? What if you've got a
lonely-heart holly that never bears fruit?
So you don't end up with two gentlemen
sharing, or a couple of spinsters, you need
to determine its sex before choosing a mate.
Get out a magnifying glass and look at the
small creamy-purple flowers. They each
contain male and female parts, but like
men's nipples and brains, the redundant
organs are undersized. Female flowers have
prominent, central ovaries surrounded by
small, aborted stamens which are shorter than
the petals. Male flowers have fully-formed
stamens, at least as long as the petals,
around squat little ovaries.

Mind the trimmings Shape up your hollies
every few years by pruning in early spring.
Remember, you will have fewer berries than
usual that autumn.

iris foetidissima

Location, location Gladdons are found throughout southern and western Europe in thickets and woodland, often on poor, chalky soil. They are tough and hard working in gardens, where they thrive equally well given dry soil in heavy shade or moist soil in full sun. To spoil them rotten, give them a rich soil in dappled shade.

Good neighbours The foliage contrasts well with other tough evergreens like bergenias (p.20), hellebores (p.34) and hypericums (p.136). Because plants are extremely shade-tolerant they can be grown as fillers beneath deciduous shrubs with arching stems, ready to show off their bounty come leaf-fall. Given a dark and very dry corner, *I. f.* 'Variegata' will be reliably hardy however cold your climate, and works well with aspleniums (p.18).

Propagation Divide large clumps in autumn and let nature surprise you with seedlings.

> The company wonder to find the smell of so excellent an article as a piece of roast beef, so exactly similar in a leaf of this plant.

Rev. William Hanbury (1725–1778)

Stinking iris · gladdon Let me clear the air straightaway. This hardy evergreen iris isn't really the least bit stinky or whiffy. Only if you rub one of the narrow 45cm/18in leaves very, very hard between your forefinger and thumb will there be a discernible smell of Sunday lunch. If you don't, there won't. That is all.

Gladdons gladden the heart in autumn and winter and provide useful if unspectacular clumps of arching foliage for the rest of the year. The 6cm/2½in diameter flowers appear in late spring and early summer. They are as fine-boned and shapely as many an iris but barely deign to rise above the foliage. They are so subtly shaded taupe and creamy yellow, so delicately veined maroon, that they simply blend into their surroundings. Frankly, at a distance, they're invisible. Visitors won't notice them at all unless they crawl around your garden on their hands and knees, but you'll find that their understated good looks provoke much comment in a vase. Bear in mind though that each bloom you pick means one less seedhead. Since *Iris foetidissima* is primarily grown for these amazing treats, it is well to remember the adage: pluck not the flower if you would have fruit.

The large, green, three-sided pods grow to the size of a man's thumb over the summer months before ripening towards brown in autumn. Their rinds then split apart to reveal inner sides crammed with bright orange to scarlet seeds the size of petits pois. These remain attached until the very end of winter for a long-lasting, stonking great show.

Although *I. f.* var. *lutescens* is the brightest of the yellow-flowered forms, *I. f.* var. *citrina* is a better choice. With broader leaves to 60cm/24in or so in length, everything else about it is proportionately bigger and it is far freer flowering, so you get seed capsules like navvies' thumbs, and plenty of 'em. *I. f.* 'Fructu Albo' is an interesting curiosity with white seeds. *I. f.* 'Variegata', which can be a little tender, has broad bands of cream running down one side or another of its leaves. It is a distinctive foliage plant, but it is so shy to flower it rarely sets seed.

leycesteria formosa

Himalayan honeysuckle · pheasant berry

As oriental-looking as *Dicentra spectabilis* (p.62) and equally in vogue with the Victorians, this handsome, hardy and trouble-free Nepalese shrub with three full seasons of interest is far too rarely grown today. Wonder why? I have the nagging suspicion that no one dares to speak its name. *Lay-cess-tearier* was named for William Leycester, Chief Justice of Bengal, in the Danish botanist Nathaniel Wallich's *Plantae Asiaticae Rariores* (1830–1832). In no time at all serendipity and the common tongue corrupted this mouthful to the poetic and curiously descriptive Elisha's tears, an epithet now sadly fallen from use.

Pendulous 10cm/4in flower spikes are borne at the ends of the stems from mid to late summer. What makes them so striking are the claret-coloured whorls of sharply pointed bracts. The creamy-white tubular flowers themselves peep out from beneath these just a few at a time, opening in slow succession from the broad bases of the spike down to its narrow tip, leaving rounds of juicy, plum-red berries fattening in their wake. Plants reach their apotheosis in autumn when the bracts are a deep and regal purple, when ripe-to-bursting berries are glossy and dark, like oiled blackcurrants, and when every single, dangling spike hangs fully developed, stretched under its own weight – long, luscious and supremely opulent. To appreciate them fully, I suggest you cut a few stems for indoors, stripping off all the leaves for the best possible effect.

The pheasant berry was often grown in coverts for game birds to feed on. In a modern domestic setting it attracts all kinds of feathered friends and, by the end of autumn, it is shorn of fruit and bare of leaf. You can now savour the austere bamboo elegance of its bright, sea-green stems. They are smooth and hollow with a glaucous bloom and look beautiful all winter through. Alongside the red-stemmed *Cornus alba* 'Sibirica' (p.23) and underplanted with *Iris foetidissima* (opposite) and *Adonis amurensis* (p.16) they look a dream.

When new, dark green foliage appears in the middle of spring, *Leycesteria formosa* can look a little dull. Simply turn back the pages to find some early-interest plants to grow in the vicinity. For an extra shot of colour, send your beaters after that *rara avis L. f.* 'Golden Pheasant'. Most of its leaves, in part or in whole, show strong but irregular yellow variegation.

Soil and site Grow it wherever you like! *Leycesteria formosa* works well on the coast, tolerates lime, and is as good in full sun as in shade. In cold climates it may die back to the ground each winter but so long as your soil is well-drained new shoots will always spring up from the base. If your winters are mild, it is a valuable shrub for heavy and inhospitable clay.

Pruning For shapely specimens with good stem colour, cut plants almost to the ground at the end of winter. In anticipation of this ordeal, feed them generously in autumn with a ripe mulch of something rich, well-rotted and nourishing.

Boring botany In case you're interested, the genus *Leycesteria* belongs to the Caprifoliaceae family. Unlikely as it seems, it is a honeysuckle relative.

Propagation Keep an eye out for seedlings as the hollow stems don't lend themselves to cuttings. An established stand can be split in autumn with a sharp spade and a cast-iron back.

nerine bowdenii

Dry humus The belt-and-braces approach to success is to grow nerines in the rain-shadow at the foot of a tall, sunny wall and to mix plenty of sharp grit into the soil as added insurance against waterlogging. Clumps can be lifted and divided at any time during their summer holidays, but they generally flower better when a little congested, so don't do this too often. The top third of each bulb should show above ground so they can all ripen ready for autumn in the hot summer sunshine. In extremely cold climates, a thick dry mulch of bark chips or bracken can be laid down temporarily for insulation in the middle of winter.

Comfrey extract Potash-rich liquid feeds are enormously beneficial to nerines when their foliage is in active growth in spring. Make one at home simply by steeping as many comfrey leaves as you can gather in a covered bucket of water. Strain some of this foul-smelling slurry over the bulbs once a week, diluting it a little first if it seems especially potent. If you've got any to spare, give a wee dram to your crown imperials. The best variety of comfrey to grow for this purpose is *Symphytum* x *uplandicum* 'Bocking 14'.

Nerine There was a certain brand of lozenge-shaped biscuit in my childhood that had a very dry, crunchy base with a thick layer of shiny, glistening icing on top. They were a particular treat and were only to be served at birthday parties unless your parents were as rich as Croesus. After the cheese and pineapple chunks on sticks, after the sausages on sticks, the quartered scotch eggs and the potted meat sandwiches, these chemically enhanced dainties would be handed round alongside nasty fondant fancies as a prelude to trifle. We then played musical chairs, pinned tails on donkeys and passed parcels for all we were worth, before being driven or walked somewhat queasily home.

Try as I might to draw a veil over those wild years of dissipation, memories come flooding back whenever I see *Nerine bowdenii* in bloom. The reason? Their twirly, candy pink petals contain tiny opalescent cells that make them twinkle and sparkle, just like that longed-for sugar frosting.

Half a dozen or so faintly sweet, yet muskily scented flowers are carried in delicate rounded umbels to 15cm/6in across on strong, dark green scapes, which can be anywhere between 30–60cm/12–24in in height. These spectacular inflorescences rarely poke their heads above ground before early autumn, so are prized all the more for their apparent anachronism. It is as if the bulbs, during their summer dormancy, soak up the very essence of that season to save it for the next. The open blooms are incredibly long-lasting and although nerines make tempting cut flowers, they remain in excellent condition outdoors almost until the onset of winter. With nerves of steel and hot South African blood in their veins, they die back only when they're good and ready to. For them, a late autumn frost is a shower of diamonds, not a hangman's noose. The strappy 30cm/12in or so leaves only emerge when the flowers are gone and fatten the bulbs from late winter to the end of spring, when the plants take a well-deserved break.

Of the 30 or so species in the genus, only *N. bowdenii* can be regarded as winter hardy. It survives freezing temperatures down to -15°C, just so long as it is given a dry and free-draining site. For the very pink of perfection, grow *N. b.* 'Mark Fenwick' which is an especially large and vigorous variety.

left: *Nerine bowdenii* 'Alba'; right: *Nerine bowdenii*

Distantly related to those magnificent spring-blooming pot plants the amaryllis and the clivia, this just has to be the most extraordinary bulb it is possible to grow out of doors.

physalis alkekengi

Spread a little happiness Chinese lanterns do well enough anywhere, but to reach their full potential they need a soil that never dries out during the late spring to summer growing period. Contented plants quickly rampage by means of underground runners, so lift and divide them every couple of years, late in autumn or early in spring. Replant the best bits and give the rest away to friends.

Light up your garden A mixed planting of *Euonymus alatus* (p.133), *Iris foetidissima* (p.138), *Physalis alkekengi* and *Phytolacca americana* (opposite) in an informal corner of the garden provides a fantastic blast of colour in autumn, particularly in the vicinity of a witch hazel (p.33) or Japanese maple (p.118) whose leaves turn butter yellow or fiery orange.

Cheer up your home Flower arrangers should harvest stems when the calyces are fully expanded then hang them upside down to dry in an airy shed or attic. The leaves come clean away when the bunches are bone dry. Older, skeletonized specimens make an effective contrast in vases. These can be whitened, if you like, in a mild solution of bleach. They combine well with honesty (p.69), corkscrew twiglets of *Corylus avellana* 'Contorta' (p.24) and dried stalks of, you guessed it, *Iris foetidissima* (p 138).

It hath the fruyte in little seed vesselles lyke unto bladders round and rede like golde.

William Turner (c1508–1568)

Chinese lanterns · winter cherry Given ample moisture at the roots, the rather gangling stems of this hardy herbaceous perennial grow to 75cm/30in tall and sprout coarsely textured 12cm/5in long mid-green leaves the shape of broad arrowheads. Yellowish-white, bell-shaped blooms with starry mouths appear amongst the foliage in the middle and latter part of summer, but your jaw won't drop in amazement at their size or their beauty. Plants are best tucked well out of sight at the back of a border. They should be grown through twiggy sticks for support unless held more or less upright by their neighbours. So far, so dull. Come autumn though, as their companions fade away and the stems turn woody and hard, you are in for a treat.

After each flower is pollinated, its calyx of fused sepals slowly inflates into a ribbed bladder or lantern to protect the resulting berry. As the calyces bellow out to 5cm/2in, they ripen from green to a bright orange red that contrasts beautifully with the yellow autumn foliage. It's hard to decide whether to leave them in situ or to take them indoors in their prime

Physalis alkekengi is indigenous to south-east Europe and western Asia, but in gardens it is surpassed by the form from northern China, Korea and Japan known as *P. a.* var. *franchetii*. This larger and more vigorous plant grows to 1m/3ft tall and has bigger, more pointed lanterns to 7cm/3in long. *P. a.* var. *franchetii* 'Variegata' has leaves irregularly, but deeply margined in cream and randomly splotched light green. It deserves a prominent position in the border, but the variegation can become sun-scorched so give it dappled shade for preference. The largest seedheads of all belong to *P. a.* var. *f.* 'Gigantea'.

In winter, the papery walls of the calyces slowly dissolve leaving skeletonized caskets through which the fat and now fully ripened orange to scarlet berries can be clearly seen. These are not for eating. The genus belongs to the tricky Solanaceae family which includes daturas, deadly nightshade and mandrake on the one hand, aubergines, peppers, potatoes and tomatoes on the other, with tobacco somewhere in between. The edible physalis or Cape gooseberry is the tropical South American *P. peruviana*.

phytolacca americana

Pokeweed · red ink plant · pigeon-berry This
untamed beauty for the wild garden or the wilder gardener,
grows stems to 2m/6½ft tall in a season – double that for well-
established clumps in really rich moist soil. The abundant mid-
green, lance-shaped leaves can be up to 30cm/1ft long and the
huge taproots go about 1m/3ft deep. Depending on your
temperament, it's either an ineradicable weed or one of the
greatest thrills you can have in a bed.

The generic name derives simply enough from the Greek
phyton, a plant, and *lac*, French for the artist's pigment crimson
lake (which in fact is obtained by crushing the Indian scale insect
Lacifer lacca – so don't go licking your paintbrush). From mid
summer onwards, this hardy North American species bears
upright, white flower panicles, which turn into thick and
decadent spikes of autumn berries. These slowly ripen, like some
debauched corn-on-the-cob, from green, through pink and
maroon, to glistening purple-black. All the while, the stems blush
ruby red and the foliage takes on a rich variety of tints long
before plants die back to the ground for winter. Now for a darker
and more complex note…

Birds and animals love to pick at the fruit. Don't follow their
example. Though the berries have been baked in pies, made into
jams, and their bloody juice has been used to colour wine, they
are chocker with toxins. Dried kidney beans must be boiled for at
least ten minutes if they are not to cause severe stomach upsets.
Stewed rhubarb stems are delicious, but their leaves cause
irreparable muscle and kidney damage. Pokeweed too demands
respect, and must remain the exclusive preserve of those with a
long family tradition of using the stuff. Yes, the young shoots
have been eaten like asparagus, but you must take care not to
harvest the least portion of root and to boil them in a change of
water, or you'll be the last of your line. Yes, the young leaves
have been served as spring greens. And some lovely services have
been held afterwards. I want you to be an adventurous gardener,
not a foolhardy cook.

Soil and site The deep-penetrating roots of
Phytolacca americana like a good, deep soil.
It needn't be especially rich, but the damper
the growing conditions, the more spectacular
your plants. They look fantastic in association
with *Arundo donax* (p.87) and *Eupatorium
purpureum* (p.134) on watersides; on a
smaller scale, they are exciting specimens for
the back of a border. They are happy in full
sun or dappled shade.

Propagation Clumps can be divided with
a lot of hard work in late autumn or early
spring, but it's easier to keep a look out for
seedlings. If you get a bumper crop, simply
hoe down the surplus.

Common-sense Remember to handle all
plants with respect. What about the things you
grow that no-one has warned you about yet?

rosa moyesii

Hip, hip, hoorah! Robinson was wrong. Breeders have produced excellent variations on a theme. *Rosa moyesii* f. *rosea* has pink flowers and abundant hips. *R. m.* var.*fargesii* is similar in bloom with larger hips though fewer of them. *R. m.* 'Geranium' has bright red flowers, large hips and a compact habit. *R. m.* 'Highdownensis' has clusters of pale-centred, soft crimson blooms. *R. m.* 'Hillieri' has delicately scented, brownish-red flowers that are the darkest of the lot. *R. m.* 'Sealing Wax' has bright pink petals and especially brilliant hips. They might not surpass the original, but they're certainly as good.

General care *R. moyesii* will tolerate poorer soils than many roses, but still appreciates a generous annual mulch. It requires little in the way of pruning besides a light tidying of awkward growth late in autumn. Remove the odd, elderly cane on well-established specimens to keep them light and airy.

Rosa moyesii This tall-growing, rather open and arching shrub eventually attains a height and top spread of around 3m/10ft, but takes up comparatively little ground space. Its size demands a position at the back of a flower bed, so its shortage of fragrance really isn't an issue, and while most roses have just one season of interest, *Rosa moyesii* has at least two.

The 6cm/2½in diameter single blooms are composed of five overlapping, deep, crimson petals with a bright central ring of golden-yellow stamens. They appear in the early and middle part of summer on numerous short spurs along the upper parts of the canes. Plants would be grown for these alone, but the double whammy comes with the spiny orange to scarlet hips, which are early to ripen and such a striking and long-lasting garden feature. Glowing against the finely cut bluish-green foliage, they are a brilliant contrast to the predominantly purple or pink flowered perennials growing beneath them in the first half of autumn. Then after leaf-fall, their shapeliness silhouetted against the sky, they perfectly echo and complement the colours of the seedheads and berries to be found at their feet. The hips persist into the first half of winter and look magnificent on frosty mornings, as their surface spikes act like magnets for ice crystals.

Reliably hardy, *R. moyesii* was noted on the Chinese border with Tibet in 1894, but only introduced to the West in 1903 by the plant-hunter E. H. Wilson. He named it for his host at the time, the Reverend J. Moyes of the China Inland Mission, and it received immediate acclaim.

Wilson's plant was in fact a selected form of a very variable species; wild specimens usually have deep pink flowers. Garden seedlings generally revert to type, but what is especially disappointing is that they are often sterile, so produce no hips. Named varieties and crosses should be perpetuated by taking cuttings as for the spring-flowering *R. banksiae* (p.80). Leave hybridizing to the experts.

The most strikingly beautiful rose that has come to us for many years. It is splendid in colour and vigour, with its red, bottle-shaped fruits… Men talk of getting fine things by crossing this, but you will never get anything so good.

William Robinson (1838–1935)

schizostylis coccinea

Kaffir lily Found wild on muddy riverbanks in the Drakensberg mountains of southern Africa, the kaffir lily's luscious looks belie a hardy and ox-like constitution. Although in cultivation since at least 1864 it has never quite caught on, probably because pessimistic gardeners rarely look for flowers beyond the end of summer. It is time to rectify the oversight. Though *Schizostylis* is a genus of but a single species, the vivacious and eye-catching blooms come in a variety of good, clear colours. If you can provide the right growing conditions the question isn't which one to grow, but how many?

In botanical terms the narrow, virtually evergreen, sword-shaped leaves and rhizomatous roots give the game right away: this isn't a lily at all but a member of the iris family – it occasionally goes by the more descriptive soubriquet 'crimson flag'. Visually speaking, kaffir lilies are 'just right'; neither so weedy as crocosmias nor quite so brash as gladioli, their late-blooming lustrous orange-to-scarlet spikes are distinguished additions to the autumn border. They are also an excellent source of cut flowers for the home, being incredibly long-lasting in water often surviving for as long as a fortnight.

Individual flowers are shaped like wide-open crocuses and there are around 12 on each 60cm/2ft stem. The flowers of the species are 3cm/1¼in across, on the slightly tender white *Schizostylis coccinea* f. *alba* they're a fraction daintier. Heartier cultivars with flowers 5–6cm/2–2½in across include the blustering bright red 'Major' (syn. 'Grandiflora'), orange-pink 'Sunrise' (syn. 'Sunset') and mid-pink 'Jennifer'. The hotter and sunnier the summer, the longer the flowering season; prolong it with your own fair hands by deadheading regularly. For a really extended show try 'Viscountess Byng', which blooms so late its 3cm/1¼in flowers are often caught by frost unless craftily cut for indoor use first. If you really want to outwit the elements, small clumps potted up in spring will flower right through winter if moved into a cool greenhouse in mid autumn.

below: *Schizostylis coccinea* 'Mrs Hegarty'

Wet and warm As their native habitat would lead you to expect, kaffir lilies need a nutrient-rich soil, which is moist yet well drained. If you're a devil with the watering can and fertilizer then anywhere will do. They stand up well to heavy clay, but don't push your luck in a really cold climate as sodden winters lead to root rot. They do best of all when planted in a warm part of the garden where the flowers are sheltered from cold winds and where the early morning sun can't shine on them. Insulate the crowns against severe frost with a thick organic mulch once flowering is over. Better safe than sorry.

Lift and separate Blooming deteriorates with overcrowding, so lift and divide mature stands every three to four years in spring.

sedum

Stonecrop Four hundred species strong, this genus of succulents is represented in one form or another in countless gardens. Judging by their appearance, you would expect all stonecrops to be tender. Most, in fact, are fully hardy. They are widely distributed in mountainous regions of the northern hemisphere, and two species in particular are of enormous value in autumn.

Sedum spectabile, commonly called the ice plant because of its very light, glaucous green foliage, is native to northern China and Korea and had long been cultivated in Japan before being introduced to the west in 1868. The slightly scalloped, oval leaves are up to 7cm/3in long and are carried in whorls around the upright, fleshy 45cm/18in stems, which form attractive clusters as wide as they are tall. In late summer and early autumn these clumps are topped with dense, flat cymes to 15cm/6in across packed with starry pink flowers. They really are astonishingly beautiful, it's just a cruel twist of fate that they put most people in mind of cauliflower and broccoli. They are copious sources of nectar, so bees and butterflies flock to them in almost ludicrous quantity. Less noticeably, they attract adult hoverflies in droves.

Their predatory larvae are of enormous importance to the health and well-being of your garden as they wolf down greenfly like there's no tomorrow. *S. s.* 'Album', along with 'Snow Queen' and 'Stardust', has white flowers; *S. s.* 'Iceberg' has especially pale leaves too. *S. s.* 'Brilliant' is a very bright magenta pink. *S. s.* 'Carmen' or *S. s.* 'Meteor' have darker, purplish blooms, while *S. s.* 'Septemberglut' has the richest colour of all.

Sedum telephium, often referred to as orpine, is an altogether lankier species with stems to 60cm/24in tall and opposite leaves, each pair at right angles to the last. Its cymes are smaller and looser, so less vegetable-like. Its many cultivars cover the same range of flower colour, but two are outstanding for their dark purple stems and foliage: *S. t.* subsp. *maximum* 'Atropurpureum' has light pink blooms, those of *S. t.* 'Munstead Red' are reddish-bronze.

Sedum 'Herbstfreude', better known as 'Autumn Joy' is a hybrid of the two species, combining the height of *S. telephium* and the clout of *S. spectabile*. This classic plant can grow to 1m/3ft tall with umbels 20cm/8in in diameter. The pink flowers mature to a deep rusty red.

Lean and mean Sedums grown on rich soils easily become top heavy, with their outer stems keeling over sideways under the weight of the flowerheads. Plants on a restricted diet are stockier and more robust, forming dense mounds that can look after themselves without the need for ugly staking. Good drainage is essential too, especially if your winters are cold and wet, when the roots are susceptible to rot. If your ground is starved, dry and stony then conditions are perfect. If you've been cultivating a lovely, rich moisture-retentive soil for years then hard luck, you'll have to dig in lots of coarse grit at planting time. You can't give sedums too much sun or too little water, so they make good subjects for absent-minded container gardeners.

Routine care Don't be in too much of a rush to tidy plants up when their stems die and dry off. From the practical point of view, the stems are best left in situ over winter to protect the crowns from frost.

Propagation Lift and divide clumps in spring when you can just see the new season's shoots at ground level. Shocking as this sounds, you can also yank out odd stems in early summer, stick them somewhere dry and shady for a couple of days while their wounds heal, then poke them into the ground where you want them to grow.

Pests If slugs are a nuisance, your plants are in too moist a soil. Vine weevils home in on the roots if you grow sedums in pots of peaty compost. Use a loam-based medium instead.

left: *Sedum spectabile* 'Meteor'; right: *S. telephium* subsp. *maximum* 'Atropurpureum'

tricyrtis formosana

Which spot? The cooler your climate, the more open and sunny a site you should choose to induce early flowering. Otherwise you'll kiss half your buds goodbye when they croak it in the frost. The soil should be moist throughout the growing season but free-draining enough to guard against winter wet. The more open-textured or leafy it is, the more your plants will be reminded of home.

Hibernation Whether plants die back in their own good time or are suddenly cut to the ground, it is wise to insulate the roots as soon as you are able with a generous organic mulch, which will also feed the soil ready for spring.

Spawning Large, well-established clumps can be lifted and divided at the very end of winter just before plants start into growth.

Toad lily Nothing like so large or showy as many members of the Liliaceae family, toad lilies nevertheless deserve close inspection for the orchid-like quality of their delicately speckled blooms. They have six fleshy 'petals', botanically sepals, the outer three of which have bulging bases – hence the name *Tricyrtis*, from the Greek *kyrtos*, meaning convex. There are around 16 species in the genus, distributed from the Himalayas south to the Philippines. While the more common specific epithet *formosa* means handsome or finely formed, which this plant most certainly is, *formosana*, relating to Formosa, actually tells us that it is native to Taiwan.

This hardy perennial grows from short creeping rhizomes and is generally found naturally in light, dappled shade in lush woodland settings. The softly hairy stems would attain a height of 1m/3ft or so but they always arch gracefully under the weight of their leaves. Dark green and splashed maroon, these are shiny and lance-shaped growing to around 12cm/5in long. They have no stalks, so clasp directly to the stems, nudging them into gentle zig-zags.

The starry flowers measure no more than 3cm/1¼in from tip to tip and don't appear until autumn, so late in cold areas that some buds can be frosted before they have a chance to bloom. They are held in loose, branching cymes and open just a few at a time. The body colour of these waxy blooms ranges from white through pink to purple, with the yellow-throated sepals heavily freckled inside in richer tones from carmine to deep chocolate brown. Even the prominent central style and sometimes the filaments are spotted.

In large, wild gardens *Tricyrtis formosana* can be tucked away into any number of shady nooks where it can box and cox with bluebells. In smaller, informal gardens where space is at a premium you might find it dull in summer. The solution is to hem in the developing foliage with seedlings of Himalayan balsam (p.97). Remove them sharply after flowering so you don't miss out on the understated charm of this strange autumn treat.

Spring, the young morn, and Summer, the strong noon,
Have dreamed and done and died for Autumn's sake.

Richard le Gallienne (1866–1947)

vitis coignetiae

Crimson glory vine Though its spelling is a nightmare, the pronunciation trips easily enough off the tongue once you have the trick of it. Named coin-yeti-ee for a shadowy Madame Coignet who carried seeds home to France from Japan in 1875, this spectacular relative of the common grape can be difficult to propagate too – unless you know the secret – so it remains very much a collector's and connoisseur's plant to this day. *C'est dommage*. Once you've found one, and asked for it nicely, *Vitis coignetiae* is simplicity itself to grow.

You know you're in the land of giants as soon as growth bursts from the flaky grey-brown stems early in spring. The finely-toothed leaves quickly develop into great rounded hearts about 30cm/12in in diameter. Though they have the three to five lobes characteristic of all vines in the genus, these are very indistinct compared with the wine-grower's *Vitis vinifera*. Their mid-green upper surfaces are coarse to the touch and pucker between deeply impressed veins; the undersides are a light scurfy brown.

Wild specimens clamber to the tops of forest trees where they spread themselves luxuriantly through the branches. In gardens they are easily kept within bounds by regular pruning to establish a permanent woody framework, and mature plants that have always been cut hard back produce especially large leaves.

In spring and summer the glory vine has a compelling presence by sheer dint of scale, but in autumn it delivers a thumping great wallop of colour which is an absolute knock-out. Overall, as the green life in the plant returns to its roots, the foliage assumes a deep purple-bronze sheen which reddens to crimson and scarlet then mellows to orange and yellow.

Individual leaves join the pageant at different times and speeds according to age and exposure to sun, the tracery of veins often picked out in contrast to their main apparel. Riotous yet elegiac, this harlequinade is the season's grand finale, and when the last player tumbles away, the horticultural stage is set once again for winter.

Soil and site *Vitis coignetiae* does well enough anywhere, but the best autumn colour comes from specimens grown in full sun in neutral to slightly alkaline soil. A lot of moisture produces leaves which, though larger, have less autumn impact.

Pruning and training Only do this in the ice-cold dead of winter, or the sap will bleed profusely. Develop a restrained network of well spaced thick old stems and cut vigorous young stalks back to a leaf node or two of this each year. Remove weak and crowded growth completely. The main framework needs tying to its support, but the annual leafy growth clings by means of tendrils.

No big deal Cuttings won't strike in winter, and it's dangerous to remove wood at any other time. Layering of long or low-lying stems in autumn works a treat, just don't snick the bark where it lies in the ground.

Fee-fi-fo-fum If you're wary of giants, try *Vitis vinifera* 'Purpurea'. Its fruit, like the glory vine's, is unpalatable, but the 15cm/6in leaves turn from claret in spring to cassis in autumn. For a muscat-scented dessert grape try *V. v.* 'Perle de Czaba' instead. *Votre santé*!

Conclusion

Growth is the only evidence of life.

Cardinal John Henry Newman (1801–1890)

YOUR GARDEN CHANGES AND DEVELOPS WITH EVERY PASSING YEAR. WHAT IS MORE, SO DO YOU. As trees and shrubs mature they form larger and denser leaf canopies which affect the plants beneath: sun lovers might find themselves struggling in shade where once there was plenty of light, woodlanders might suddenly flourish as never before. Some perennials spread more vigorously than others and can alter the intended balance of a border – if you like the new effect then go with the flow, if not, be prepared to take remedial action. The more established a garden, the fewer toe-holds there are likely to be for seedlings of annuals and biennials – allow them to fade away if you only ever wanted them as temporary fillers, but if you've come to love them in their own right, then grub up some groundcover to give them a permanent home.

If your personal or professional life is making increasing demands on your time then for heaven's sake make greater use of tried and tested workhorses instead of experimenting with fancy-pants plants. If you find garden work a soothing distraction from worldly hustle and bustle, by all means push at the boundaries of what you think might be possible. As your tastes change, adapt your garden accordingly – why be a slave to your former self?

Once upon a time, in a faraway land, people would settle in a home and stay there forever. Today, in the here and now, many of us change jobs and move house often. New gardens bring new challenges and exciting opportunities; they can also lend continuity to our disjointed lives. By propagating plants and taking them with you it is possible to leave a perfectly-formed garden behind for someone else's enjoyment yet to carry forward memories of earlier times, of family and friends. And if gardeners can't make the world a better place for themselves and others, who can?

right: *Physalis alkekengi*

the garden in winter

Though an old man, I am but a young gardener.

Thomas Jefferson (1743–1826)

Winter stands as a portal between one gardening year and the next. It is the perfect interval for reflection upon the past and for contemplation of the future. It is also a season to be enjoyed in its own right. With so many short, dark days, which can be cold and depressing, the garden in winter, perhaps more than at any other time, should be treated as a celebration of life.

This is a quiet time, not a dead one, and there is always something stirring in a generously stocked border. Berries and seed heads remain on view until the birds peck them away or until they fall to the ground ready for germination in spring. In the first part of winter, the odd belated bloom will appear on plants that normally flower in late summer and in autumn. In the latter part, there will always be a precocious primrose or violet. Evergreens provide invaluable form and structure throughout the season, those with golden variegated leaves being especially bright and cheerful as they give the impression of being bathed in warm, yellow sunlight. But is all this enough? Of course not.

These incidental pleasures of the cold months are well and good, but do yourself a favour: look at all the blank, dreary spaces in between them, then visualize these gaps filled with plants from the first part of this book. Better? I hope so. Wrap up warm and take a leisurely snoop around your neighbourhood, or stroll around the park, or visit a private garden open to the public. Find your inspiration, then do something about it.

However much people pack their gardens with colour from spring to autumn, they rarely *plan* for winter. Be the exception to the rule. Put the names of the plants you like in your diary or notebook then try to get hold of at least some of them during the course of the year. If you have recently moved house, or if you're not overly familiar with the plants in your garden, a helpful trick is to sprinkle sand over especially large barren patches then see what comes up later on. Where nothing has appeared by late spring, get your bucket and spade ready, go shopping, and get planting!

the garden in spring

Spring is sooner recognized by plants than man.

Chinese proverb

Spring is irrepressible. Little green outbursts and exclamations herald its arrival – then in no time at all the garden positively burgeons with fresh new growth. It is a season of youthful optimism, and a promise of things to come. Today's quivering buds are tomorrow's blooms, while slowly unfurling foliage lends sustenance to the flowers of summertime.

It is important to start the season as you mean to go on. Make your mind up about the effects you want to achieve in the garden, then stick to your guns. This is the time when everyone rushes off to the nearest garden centre and buys anything they can lay their hands on, just so long as it's in flower. There's no harm in this if you repeat the procedure in each succeeding season; if not, you need to exercise a little self-discipline. By all means extend your range of springtime blooms, but keep eyes in the back of your head for winter-interest plants being sold off cheap and invest some of your savings in plants that will mature in summer and autumn, so you can reap dividends the whole year round. Whatever you do, don't lug home full-blown pots of left-over bulbs: you can choose and plant better specimens yourself for much less money later on. Many a mickle makes a muckle – as I believe they say in Scotland.

Garden plants aren't the only things bursting into new life. Pluck out weed seedlings as soon as you recognise them and squish any pests that cross your path. Slugs are suddenly a lot less sluggish, so protect special treasures with a handful or two of sharp grit or a scattering of dried holly leaves. Nip outbreaks of greenfly in the bud. A few aphid mouthfuls now can jeopardize a whole shoot's future; once growth is well underway, damage is mostly cosmetic. A little extra vigilance now saves a lot of heartache later on. As soon as your garden has gained the upper hand, just relax and learn to enjoy your wildlife. Weeds can't get much of a toe-hold once the ground is smothered with your chosen plants; pests won't be too great a problem if you maintain a sense of proportion. Live and let live.

the garden in summer

The desire, the capacity, is an instinct, the love of flowers is innate, a remembrance of Eden.

Dean Samuel Reynolds Hole (1819–1904)

Summer contains almost three seasons in one. Late spring merges seamlessly into early summertime; the garden then pulsates with vibrancy and intense colour, before slowly turning blowsy and mellow to make the transition to autumn.

Maintain your garden in optimum condition by using a little imagination to anticipate its needs. Life is far simpler this way. Though the days are longer, always aim to cut your work as short as possible so you can simply sit back and enjoy the fruits of your labours while idly musing on future improvements. Thin out self-sown biennials before they become overcrowded. If you use brushwood to support clumps of tall-growing perennials, you won't have to stake each flower stem individually later on. Don't water early in the season unless it's absolutely necessary, or you'll be a martyr to your hosepipe for months ahead. Do remove spent flower heads regularly to eke as many blooms as possible from

each plant. Note any clumps that have become tired or overcrowded, then lift and divide them in autumn or spring – they'll flower all the better the following year. Earmark visible gaps for planting up with new shrubs or perennials, for transplanting divisions and rooted cuttings into, or for filling with seedlings from elsewhere. Nose around for patches of bare ground concealed by neighbouring foliage, which can be planted up with bulbs for autumn, winter or spring.

Always weigh up your priorities, and never create more jobs than you can comfortably handle. You will get more pleasure from slowly enhancing a well-tended border than from racing into some elaborate scheme that quickly spirals beyond your control.

It's a sad garden and a sadder gardener that can't spare a bunch of flowers for the house or for a friend. Summer is a generous season and it's a shame not to enter into the spirit.

the garden in autumn

Nature is reluctant and loth to die, or to be kept down, or to be overcome, or to be in subjection, or readily to be subdued.

Thomas à Kempis (1380–1471)

Autumn is more than just an afterthought to summer. Some of the deepest and richest colours of the year are now found concentrated in leaves, in fruits and in the flowers of late-blooming plants. The sun is lower in the sky and the quality of light, as the nights begin to draw in, is noticeably different. The dazzling brightness of summertime, which sometimes makes flowers seem washed-out and faded, is replaced by a soft, warm glow that brings out previously unnoticed subtleties. It also makes the shocking pinks, the scarlets and the purples so unique to autumn look all the more outrageous.

Increasing moisture in the air brings out the earthiness of the soil and the sweet, nutty smell of fallen leaves. Wisps of bonfire smoke are carried on the breeze. Butterflies and bees feast on the last of the nectar, darting birds feed on seeds and berries. This is a season to savour.

Don't rush to tidy everything away. Not only do the stems of perennials and the drying leaves of grasses have a charm of their own, they insulate each plant's crown from frost. The longer they are left in place, the more goodness returns to their roots and the easier they are to twist clean away late in winter or early in spring. This relaxed approach ensures the base of each plant is free of debris when new growth begins. Fastidiously cutting everything back in autumn can actually be harmful; the cluster of stubble it leaves behind can harbour pests and diseases as it slowly rots away. Planting bulbs is a more rewarding occupation.

If your winters are cold, pruning is best left until the worst weather has passed. Otherwise, get out your secateurs and get to work. If you've got any new acquisitions still hanging around in pots, you should be thoroughly ashamed of yourself. Put them in the ground straightaway.

get planting

Cicely: When I see a spade, I call it a spade.
Gwendolen: I am glad to say that I have never seen a spade.
It is obvious that our social spheres have been widely different.

Oscar Wilde (1854–1900) *The Importance of Being Earnest*

Whatever the season, any plant is better off in the ground than out of it, so the sooner a new acquisition gets stuck in, the better. Procrastinate and you're the victim of a simple but widespread misunderstanding. The notion of a correct 'planting time' harks back to the days when nurseries used only to dig up their stock and send out whole plants or divisions in spring or autumn, their roots temporarily bundled in damp hessian. Lightweight flowerpots and composts have more or less put paid to all that; you can now buy container-grown specimens at the height of summer and, if you must, in the depths of frost too. Once you've made your purchase, there's no point whatsoever in letting it hang around unless recent rain has made the ground so wet and claggy as to make digging impossible. Fear no more the heat o' the sun, plants have greater reserves of water to draw on the sooner they're let loose in cool, damp earth. Ignore the furious winter's rages, garden soil provides better insulation for roots than thin-walled plastic pots ever can.

To get a plant off to a flying start you need to settle it comfortably in a welcoming home. Before doing anything else, soak the containerised plant in a bucket of water to wet the rootball thoroughly. Then, assuming you've chosen the optimum location, the next step is to excavate as large a hole as possible – three times the width and twice the depth of the pot isn't too big. 'Dig a shilling hole for a penny plant' has got to be the best gardening motto of all time. Fill it with water from your bucket and allow this to seep away as you enrich your mound of soil with well-rotted compost or manure. If you need to drive in a stake for support, now is the time to get it as deep as possible. With the plant still in its container to keep root disturbance to a minimum, lower it into the hole to determine how much of your new, improved soil needs tipping back in to get the neck of the plant at ground level. As you do this, scrape the top 1cm/½in of soil from the top of the pot into the bottom of the hole. This gets rid of unwanted weedlings and seeds. Back fill the hole to the appropriate level. Then tap the plant out of its pot and loosen any congested roots with your fingers before finally putting it in

position. Fill in around the sides, then softly firm the soil to a little below ground level and form a reservoir around the hole with the remaining earth. Water the plant in with a fine spray from a full can then, when the last drops have drained away, draw the rim of dry soil gently over the wet surface to act as a moisture-retaining mulch. Add an organic mulch if you wish, but leave a healthy breathing space around the plant's stems. All you need to do now is step back and admire your handiwork.

Getting your plants

To begin transforming your garden, you have to get hold of your precious raw materials. Easier said than done? Not at all!

Where there's muck, there's brass. Big business realized long ago that home improvement embraces both house and garden, so if there's a hangar of a DIY store near you, it will probably have a pretty good garden centre round the back. If they've got a plant you want, chances are they'll have it in abundance, so take your time picking over the pots to choose the very best specimen on display. Because operations like this buy in bulk, their goods are cheap, but the range on offer at any given moment is pretty restricted. Fresh seasonal consignments are always coming in though, so repeat visits can be very rewarding.

Independent garden centres are usually located on the outskirts of towns, where small businesses find land more affordable. They carry a wider range of flowers, shrubs and trees, and because their staff are focused purely on plants, they are a lot more forthcoming with help and advice. If you can't find what you're after, don't be afraid to ask. This kind of set-up orders stock in relatively small quantities and can often get a plant in especially for you. If not, they may be able to suggest a nursery you might try direct.

Nurseries actually propagate and grow the plants they sell. At one end are the vast concerns that only sell wholesale to the trade. At the other are tiny cottage industries run more for love than money. Nurseries open to the public are usually found in the depths of the countryside and can form part of a day out. Large ones woo families with cream teas and gifte shoppes; small ones often arise as adjuncts to the owners' private gardens, which you are allowed to wander round at leisure.

Once you are actually seen to be making an effort, you will find that other local gardeners not only advise (take on board what you want to, smile politely at the rest), but also offer cuttings and divisions of their own plants. We're a generous bunch by nature, but canny too, so propagate the treasures you've already accumulated if you want to keep the ball rolling.

When you're really stuck and just can't track a plant down in person you might have to send off for it. Mail order is offered by good, indifferent and downright appalling nurseries; unfortunately you only find out which you're dealing with once you're saddled with your purchase. As a general rule, the quality of the plants is in inverse proportion to the glossiness of the catalogues. Gardening magazines are a good source of addresses, and they also give listings of horticultural shows. These are well worth a visit.

Not only do large events attract a wide range of commercial exhibitors, they also act as showcases for specialist plant societies, which often have stalls selling plants grown by their members. If you develop a taste for a particular genus, there's bound to be an organisation full of like-minded souls. In the first instance, to broaden your gardening horizons, I suggest you contact your national society.

Royal Horticultural Society
80 Vincent Square
London SW1P 2PE

Irish Garden Plant Society
c/o National Botanical Garden
Glasnevin
Dublin 9

American Horticultural Society
7931 East Boulevard Drive
Alexandria
VA 22308

Botanical Society of South Africa
Kirstenbosch
Claremont
Cape Town 7735

The Organisation of Plant Collections in Australia
c/o Royal Botanic Garden
Birdwood Avenue
South Yarra
Victoria 3141

In the UK the Royal Horticultural Society annually issues *The Plant Finder*, a comprehensive listing of plants in commerce with a directory of suppliers. In the USA, the American Horticultural Society offers a 'Plants Wanted' Service.

index

acknowledgements

Author's Acknowledgements

Sharon Amos; Neil Andrews; Veronique Baxter; Daniela Bernadelle; Liz Boyd; Martin Breese; Brigitte Bunnell; Guy Cooper; Lorraine Dickey; Nabil Abou-Hamad; Orlando Hamilton; Vickie Hamilton; Karen Higgs; Georgina Hohler; Benois von Kitting; Heidi Lascelles; Steve McCarthy; Sybella Marlow; Geraldine Murray; Jilliana Ranicar-Breese; Edward Ratley; Anke Reichelt; Anne Robbins; Diana Ross; Marie Saba; Finbar Saunders; Valerie Scriven; Liz Seeber; Megan Smith; Catharine Snow; Sue Storey; Ruth Swindon; Curtice Taylor; Gordon Taylor; Marie-Françoise Valéry; and extra special thanks to Katey Day and Margaret Parry.

Publisher's Acknowledgements

The publisher would like to thank the following photographers and agencies for their kind permission to reproduce the photographs in this book.

1 Marcus Harpur/Harpur Garden Library (Harvey's Garden Plants Bradfield, Suffolk); 2–3 Marianne Majerus; 4 left Clive Nichols; 4 right Andrew Lawson; 5 left Tim Spence/The Garden Picture Library; 5 right S & O Mathews Photography; 6 Clive Nichols (Piet Oudolf); 7–9 Jerry Harpur/ Harpur Garden Library; 10 Mark Bolton; 13 Andrew Lawson; 14 Clive Nichols; 15 Mark Bolton/The Garden Picture Library; 16 Marianne Majerus; 17 Mark Bolton; 18 S & O Mathews Photography; 19 Andrew Lawson; 20 S & O Mathews Photography; 21 Marcus Harpur/Harpur Garden Library; 22 Jerry Harpur/Harpur Garden Library; 23 S & O Mathews Photography; 24 Andrew Lawson; 25 Clay Perry; 26 Clive Nichols; 27–28 Marcus Harpur/ Harpur Garden Library; 29 Andrew Lawson; 30 Marianne Majerus; 31 Marcus Harpur/Harpur Garden Library; 32 Marianne Majerus; 33 Marcus Harpur/Harpur Garden Library; 34 Andrew Lawson; 35 Claire Davies/ The Garden Picture Library; 36 Andrew Lawson; 37 Andrea Jones; 38 Andrew Lawson; 39 Jerry Harpur/Harpur Garden Library; 40 Mark Bolton/The Garden Picture Library; 41–42 Marianne Majerus; 43 Clive Nichols; 44 John Glover/The Garden Picture Library; 45 Andrew Lawson; 46 S & O Mathews Photography; 47 Jerry Harpur/Harpur Garden Library; 48 Marianne Majerus; 49 Mark Bolton; 50 Marianne Majerus; 51 Andrew Lawson; 52 Mark Bolton; 53 Clive Nichols; 54 Jerry Harpur/Harpur Garden Library (Caerhayes, Cornwall); 55 Mark Bolton; 56 Marianne Majerus; 57 JS Sira/The Garden Picture Library; 58 Andrea Jones; 59 Jonathan Buckley; 60–61 Andrew Lawson; 62–63 Jerry Harpur/Harpur Garden Library; 64 Andrew Lawson; 65 Neil Holmes/The Garden Picture Library; 66 Jerry Harpur/Harpur Garden Library; 67 Marcus Harpur/Harpur Garden Library; 68 Howard Sooley; 69 Marianne Majerus; 70 Howard Rice/The Garden Picture Library; 71 John Ferro Sims/The Garden Picture Library; 72 Clive Nichols; 73–74 Andrew Lawson; 75 Mark Bolton; 76 S & O Mathews Photography; 77 Andrew Lawson; 78 Mark Bolton; 79 Neil Holmes/ The Garden Picture Library; 80 Clive Nichols; 81–82 Andrew Lawson; 83 Mark Bolton; 84 John Glover/The Garden Picture Library; 85 Marcus Harpur/Harpur Garden Library; 86 Howard Rice/The Garden Picture Library; 87 Jerry Hapur/Harpur Garden Library; 88–89 Marianne Majerus; 90 S & O Mathews Photography; 91 Andrew Lawson; 92 Jonathan Buckley (Beth Chatto Garden); 93 Eric Crichton/The Garden Picture Library; 94 Marcus Harpur/Harpur Garden Library; 95 Christopher Fairweather/The Garden Picture Library; 96 Marcus Harpur/Harpur Garden Library; 97 JS Sira/ The Garden Picture Library; 98 Mark Bolton/The Garden Picture Library; 99 Jonathan Buckley (Christopher Lloyd); 100 S & O Mathews Photography; 101 Brigitte Thomas/The Garden Picture Library; 102 Jerry Harpur/Harpur Garden Library; 103 Janet Sorrell/The Garden Picture Library; 104 Jerry Harpur/Harpur Garden Library; 105 Jonathan Buckley; 106 Marcus Harpur/Harpur Garden Library; 107 Andrew Lawson; 108 Marianne Majerus; 109 Neil Holmes/The Garden Picture Library; 110 Andrew Lawson; 111 Densey Clyne/The Garden Picture Library; 112 Mark Bolton; 113 Clive Nichols; 114 Andrew Lawson; 115 Jerry Harpur/Harpur Garden Library (Hermannshof, Germany); 116 Clive Nichols; 117 Andrew Lawson; 118 Alec Scaresbrook/The Garden Picture Library; 119 S & O Mathews Photography; 120 Didier Willery/The Garden Picture Library; 121 Jerry Harpur/Harpur Garden Library; 122 Chris Burrows/The Garden Picture Library; 123 Andrew Lawson; 124 Clive Nichols; 125 Neil Holmes/The Garden Picture Library; 126 Mark Bolton; 127 Howard Rice/The Garden Picture Library; 128 S & O Mathews Photography; 129 Sunniva Harte/The Garden Picture Library; 130 Andrew Lawson; 131 Jonathan Buckley; 132 Clive Nichols (Designer: Piet Oudolf); 133 Marianne Majerus; 134 Andrew Lawson; 135 Marianne Majerus; 136 Jerry Harpur/Harpur Garden Library; 137 S & O Mathews Photography; 138 Jerry Harpur/Harpur Garden Library; 139 Mark Bolton/The Garden Picture Library; 140 Chris Burrows/The Garden Picture Library; 141 Marianne Majerus; 142–143 Mark Bolton; 144 Howard Rice/The Garden Picture Library; 145 Jonathan Buckley; 146 Andrew Lawson; 147 Clive Nichols; 148 Howard Rice/The Garden Picture Library; 149 John Glover/The Garden Picture Library; 151 Howard Rice/The Garden Picture Library; 152 Jonathan Buckley (Designers: Sue & Wol Staines); 153 Jonathan Buckley (Designer: Christopher Lloyd); 154 Jonathan Buckley (Designer: Helen Yemm); 155 Jonathan Buckley (Designer: Helen Yemm); 156 John Glover.

Every effort has been made to trace the copyright holders. We apologise in advance for any unintentional omissions, and would be pleased to insert the appropriate acknowledgement in any subsequent edition.